# PAPERCUTS AND PLENTY

## By Elly Sienkiewicz

# Papercuts and Plenty

*Volume Three of Baltimore Beauties and Beyond*
*Studies in Classic Album Quilt Appliqué*

## By Elly Sienkiewicz

C&T PUBLISHING

Photography by Jack Mathieson, Sharon Risedorph, and through the courtesy of the contributors as noted. All photographs not otherwise credited are by the author.

Front Cover Photo: Detail from Classic Revival: Alex's Album (Quilt #6 on page 71), Group Quilt made under the author's direction, quilted by Mona Cumberledge, 1988-92. The pictured blocks were hand-appliquéd by Mary Wise Miller (portrait block), Arlene Nabor (Cherub block), Eva L. Hudson (Devon Violets for Nana block), and Shirley C. Wedd (*E Pluribus Unum*: Eagles and Oaks block). The borders were hand-appliquéd by Nonna Crook and Albertine Veenstra. Brief biographies of those who made the individual blocks are listed in "Part Three: The Quiltmakers." Inkwork by the author. Photograph by Sharon Risedorph, San Francisco.

Partial bibliographies for the *Baltimore Beauties* Series appear in *Volume I, Baltimore Album Quilts*, and *Volume II*. The concluding partial bibliography appears in *Stitched in Cloth, Carved in Stone*, the sequel to *Volume III of Baltimore Beauties and Beyond*.

Hand illustrations by Lorelei Brede
Electronic illustrations by Ginny Coull

Editing by Louise Owens Townsend
Technical editing by Joyce Engels Lytle

Book design by Riba Taylor, Sebastopol, California

Published by C&T Publishing, P.O. Box 1456, Lafayette, California 94549

ISBN 0-914881-96-5 (Hardcover)
ISBN 0-914881-90-6 (Softcover)

Library of Congress Cataloging-in-Publication Data
(Revised for vol. 3)

Sienkiewicz, Elly
Baltimore beauties and beyond.

    Vol. 3 has special title: Papercuts and plenty.
    Vol. 3 includes an index to the 9 books in the
Baltimore beauties series.
    Includes bibliographical references.
    1. Appliqué—Patterns. 2 Album quilts—Maryland—
Baltimore. 3. Patchwork—Patterns. I. Title.
II. Title: Papercuts and plenty.
TT779.S54 1989          746.44'5         89-60479
ISBN 0-914881-23-X (v. 1)
ISBN 0-914881-40-X (v. 2)
ISBN 0-914881-34-5 (v. 2 : pbk.)

We have made every attempt to properly credit the trademarks and brand names of the items mentioned in this book. We apologize to any companies that have been listed incorrectly, and we would appreciate hearing from you.

*Baltimore Beauties* is a registered trademark of Elly Sienkiewicz.
(Elly Sienkiewicz's *Baltimore Beauties* is a signature fabric line produced by P&B Textiles.)
Bernina is a registered trademark of Fritz Gegauf, Ltd.
Classic Metal Iron is a registered trademark of Black & Decker Corporation.
Con-Tact Self-Adhesive Covering is a registered trademark of United Merchants and Manufacturers, Inc.
Creative Art Products Paintstik Markers is a registered trademark of Laco Industries, Inc.
DMC Medici Wool is a registered trademark of the DMC Corporation.
Gingher Tailor-Point Scissors is a registered trademark of Gingher, Inc.
Pigma Micron and Pigma SDK are registered trademarks of the Sakura Color Products Corporation of America.
Pilot SC-UF is a registered trademark of Pilot Pen Corporation of America.
Renaissance Wool is a brand name of Sew Art International.
Warm and Natural is a trademark of Warm Products.
X-Acto is a registered trademark of Hunt Manufacturing Company.

Printed in Hong Kong
First Edition
10    9    8    7    6    5    4    3    2    1

# TABLE OF CONTENTS

*The Color Section begins on page 57.*

# ACKNOWLEDGMENTS

Fundamental to *Papercuts and Plenty* are all the needleartists who made the blocks and quilts that bring its text to life. We learned together. Without you, this book could never have been. I am forever grateful for your faith, time, talent—your buoyant enthusiasm and your friendship. I appreciate so much, as well, the generous gifts of stitching and photographs for this book. Thank you all! Thank you, too, to Elaine Fugate, Nancy Fulford, Joel and Kate Kopp of America Hurrah! and others who have shared pictures of their Baltimore Album family heirlooms and treasures from private collections. And thank you so much to my colleague, Denise Scott, who is largely responsible for the monumental task of keeping the thread of reproduction permissions and thank yous and needleartists' biographies and photo credits in a tidy, unwindable manner! Her intelligent and gracious assistance with this fifth book, now, is indeed a blessing.

Thank you to the skilled team at C&T Publishing who have brought *Volume III* to life: Louise Townsend, Joyce Lytle, Diane Pedersen, Todd and Tony Hensley—and all those on C&T's hardworking team who are my colleagues and have become my friends. Louise, long intrigued by Baltimore's Albums, worked intensively with the 1994 quiltmaker's contest essays and was so inspired by their spirit that she has begun Album-making herself. No author could be so privileged as to have a more sympathetic editor! Louise volunteered to compile the Index to the *Baltimore Beauties*® Series Patterns, Quiltmakers, and Techniques, which concludes this volume. I am so grateful for this practical gift—a gratitude that will surely be reflected by so many others in years to come. Joyce, too, whose skills have been sharpened by stitching a complex Album block, has edited the illustrations and patterns with a care that benefits us all.

Thank you to Lorelei Brede, the hand illustrator; to Ginny Coull, the electronic illustrator; and to Riba Taylor, the designer, whose expertise transformed the manuscript into a finished book. A special hail and farewell to Paulann Di Laura who served for so short a time, but with such impact, as publicist. And thanks also to Chris Dietzel who later brought her skills and talents to that task. And what better time and place to once again say Thank You to all of you at C&T, from all us Baltimore afficionadas, for the splendid Baltimore Album Revival! 1994 Show and Contest. Album makers, your quilts were magnificent!

Finally, on that personal scale where life is truly lived: Throughout all the writing, the business of teaching and authorship, the management of home and the obligations, joys, and sorrows of family—throughout all that these entail, my husband has remained the "wind beneath my wings." Thank you, Stan.

# DEDICATION

*To Katya,*

*Eileen Katherine Hamilton Sienkiewicz, last child, first daughter. You grew tall and straight, and proudly carried all those Scots and Russian family names: the grandmother's name, the great-grandmother's, and those of both the grandfathers. You were my girl-child, my dear friend, and you are leaving the nest last. This year! And oh, I do miss you already.*

# AUTHOR'S FOREWORD:

## REFLECTIONS ON AUGUST, ALBUM AMBIENCE, HORNS OF PLENTY, AND BASKETS OF BOUNTY

Tomatoes, cantaloupes, zinnias, and Silver Queen corn. I am dreaming of August's bounty, driving along the flat road to the seashore. Siren signs, crudely lettered, herald Delaware's farm country: "Lopes," they say, "Lopes Ahead," "25¢ Lopes." At the fruit stand, a cradled tomato fills my palm. The orb's weightiness surprises me. Its red is spicy hot and waxy deep. I rub the stem end, hoping for a remembered smell. A pungent herb fragrance rises on the warm air, mingles with the road dust, and wafts into my imagination. August indeed, and Washington, D.C., my hometown, is well behind me. Nature's beauty and her bounty lighten my willing spirit.

Baltimore's quiltmakers, too, were city women. Nostalgia for a receding rural way of life must also have tinged their fond depictions of fruits and flowers. Their appliquéd shapes are so simple, yet each has such evocative specifics. These telling details are "touches of genius": the heart-shaped silhouette of a greengage plum; the stem-well shadow—a printed circle, stitched—on an apple; a scattering of black seeds inked onto the pink mottled cloth of watermelon flesh. Each such observation is a keen identifier, evoking in the viewer, a thrill of recognition. We know not only the very type of plum portrayed, but we note the artist in the quiltmaker as well. These touches of genius are gifts of insight. Those women stitched like poets. Or like song writers whose perceptions are infused with passion. For their Album fruit was not simply fruit, but a metaphor for beneficence—fruit capable of sustaining both body and soul.

The era prompted a careful reading of nature. And it placed great importance on drawing both as art and as a technical skill. We've long noted such accomplished draftsmanship in many of Baltimore's Album blocks! Those who contemplated the economic facts of the Industrial Age regarded drawing as a requisite skill, comparable to computer literacy today: It was a key to getting ahead in the world. Even now, we honor that era's exceptional draftsmanship by reproducing Victorian commercial design, from embroidery scissors to lamp posts.

I spot bright basil then, its cut bunches of green, container-held, by the cash register. Vacation's ritual has begun. In August, at the beach, we feast like ancient royalty on fresh tomatoes anointed with balsamic vinegar and "extra virgin" olive oil, the serving dish decorated with sweet red onion and snips of basil leaves. Life's pace so slow, the bounty so great, that sometimes I peel the tomatoes as my Great Aunt Orpha did. To my child eyes, it was so opulent, a country thing, to pare away the edible skin, then leave its thick peels in a bucket, slop for the hogs. Opulent, also, to my adult eyes, the time spent thus to prepare tomatoes: core, peel, slice wide slabs, and alternate them— first the red fruit, then the yellow—spiraled on a plate. The pace unhurried, the pattern repeated, like a ritual. Surely love and ritual are stitched into Album squares. We, too, feed those ancient womanly needs—love and ritual—in the making of our quilts.

Stopping at a farm stand on the way to the beach is part of our vacation routine. I heft a cantaloupe, brushing off its dried mud, inhaling its perfumed summer-ripeness—pleasures unknown when we shop at home in the city. Then we gauge our lust: Will we buy a pint of peaches, a peck, or a bushel? How many can we eat without any one of them going bad? We smile conspiratorially and buy the Big One. A tableful of sawed-off milk jugs offers flowers next: cockscomb, cosmos, snapdragons, and zinnias—each Van Gogh bright. The aproned clerk wraps the stems in wet paper towels, then swaddles my chosen bunch in *The Daily Delawarian*. Like a lady's Album squares, our days at the beach shall be garlanded in flowers. Flowers fresh-cut, domestic not hot-house, not imports; flowers almost like homegrown. Ah, the longing for homemade, homegrown, to be rich with the gifts of the heart and the hand! Could the ladies of Baltimore know how they have rekindled such pleasures for us? Could they have imagined that they would?

Pressed together in a two-room cottage, we are close to these fresh altar offerings, there at the beach. For so the flowers and the bowls of fruit seem in that sparse space: still-lifes of nature's bounty; reminders for us—people of plenty—to enjoy. In the bay-bright air of Mrs. Reed's rental, we live a life stripped down. Simple pleasures uplift me there with an omnipresent sense of being blessed. Sweeping out the sand, shaking out the rugs, are communions that nourish and settle me. I try to harvest the wealth of that feeling, to name in silence my blessings and my gratitude, as though to put them up in Atlas jars for the cold months—months when life's pressures pile up stealthily, like snow. Life's cloud-shadow of fragility, the probability of loss—I think of these too, and package sunshine in my soul to light the short days.

But it is the August mood that fills me now as I consider Baltimore's Album offerings. Flowers are put forth in cornucopias, in baskets, and twined in wreaths. But amongst them are also fruits, nuts, and the occasional ornamental peppers and bunches of carrots. Both the workings of man and the bounties of nature are drawn on the Album maker's clean cloth slate. Nature's blessings are most often honored in those quilts. The glory is not to man alone.

Thus for some 22 years, my family and I (perhaps like olden-day Album makers, escaping Baltimore's heat) have driven to the Delaware shore for a week's vacation in August. In August, gratitude is on the breezes, an ethereal presence at the back of my thoughts, a live thing wrapping me lightly. I love that vacation is always the same place, a place so small it takes no care, a place so affordable we can return, a place so close that for years we thought five of us could no longer fit; then, imperceptibly decades passed and there were fewer and fewer of us again.

Just once in my childhood, my parents rented a beach cottage in Maine. My mother hungered for the ocean, and I felt her excitement at this splurge. Odd, though, how a child's memory works, for I can recall just one image from that Maine trip. In that picture, looming black pines dwarf me, their scent on the crisping salt sea air. But my mind's snapshot is a tight close-up: I sit on a swing, a lifted jar clenched in my chubby fists. I am peering into the jar to see if it is quite empty. Scraping out the peanut butter streaks, vacation's last memory, had been my packing-to-go task.

My children—now almost grown—must have their own vacation memories, all treasures from the sea. And behind their snapshots, too, will be vacation's mood: the sun that always shone, the smells of charcoal-cooking, the candy-sweetness of moon-pale corn; the hot sand we pile on our ankles late in the day, protection from the biting flies that come just when it is really time to go in for supper, anyhow. For a while now, my Album books, much of them written at the beach, have ticked off the years with a rhythm as comforting as the coming of vacation. And now *Volume III* has rolled around, the volume where, like August, the bounty of watermelons, peaches, grapes, and other Album fruits quite naturally belong. Here I hope to teach the Albums' magical papercuts and to evoke their fruitful plenty. Perhaps I'll call this "Papercuts and Plenty."

Odd Fellows (like the ancient Greeks before them) symbolized nature's bounty by an overflowing cornucopia, the horn of plenty. Often its links were colored red, yellow, and blue, the tri-colored links of Odd Fellowship's "Three-Linked Fraternity." Apples and strawberries and acorns, black-eyed susans and roses are among Baltimore's Album horn offerings. So widespread was the understanding of this symbol of plenty that after the Civil War, the cornucopia came to stand for our national Thanksgiving. It seems to me that the women Odd Fellows, the Rebekahs, had their own counterpart to the cornucopia in their basket motifs—so often shown, too, in red with touches of yellow and blue. The blessings held by both basket and horn were meant to be shared as offerings of "Friendship, Love, and Truth." For so their three-linked motto said. Slipping back into August's Baltimore mood, thinking of each stitch's bite and pull as homage to nature's beauty and bounty, cannot but lift our spirits. Cannot but recall midsummer's sweet perfume of, say, a ripened peach. Joyful, cloth-stitched songs of August praise. Warmth enough to wrap those February days.

*Elly Sienkiewicz*
*Lewes, Delaware*
*August 23, 1993*

# INTRODUCTION

## ALBUM QUILTS,
## NOT NINE PATCHES

My love of quilts began in West Virginia. There, the Nine Patch may well be the all-time favorite quilt. At least it was Great Aunt Atha's favorite, and it was she who taught me as a young mother to quilt. She gave us our first finished quilt, a green-and-white Nine Patch baby quilt for Donald, my first-born. Then as they arrived, she made a blue-and-white one for Alex; and a pink-and-white one for Katya. My great aunts and my father's Cousin Wilma had quilts, made quilts, talked quilts, and still are, for me, The Quilters. We visited them each and every August of my childhood. After my marriage, Memorial Day weekend signaled our annual visit, and does to this day. The stuff of quilts—the barnloft filled with plumply pretty feedsacks, the treadle machine, the gaslit evening sewing—were as much a part of those visits to the farm as harvesting, canning, walking the hills in the hay-fragrant heat, bathing in the creek, and breakfasting on saltines and creamed tomatoes.

Memories of the coarse, bright feedsack cloth return to me now, wafted along with kitchen smells of sugared cooking and a hint of cream, soured from the separator, which as a child I liked to spin. I remember Great Aunt Orpha's kitchen better than my own at home: I must, quite young, have begun to love history, a love inseparable from my family. The farmhouse bespoke a large family. Its living room was the original log cabin purchased mid-19th century from W. W. Duty (witnessed by words scratched in the mortar between two logs).

Three large bedrooms and a spacious farm kitchen rambled off that home center, marking the burgeoning Hamilton family of my great-grandparents' generation. Bruce, the youngest of my grandfather's siblings, and his wife, Orpha, had remained childless. Therefore, the unused bedrooms were museum-like and filled with the country needlework of many hands. These cloth artifacts fascinated me. So many memories, so many threads, fed those family and history loves. My aristocratic English-born mother, my "Vermont farmer" father, my Russian refugee husband—mine was not a simple patchwork. I needed a framework to help hold together all those details, all those sensibilities, all those kinfolk. It is not surprising then, that the quilts, which came to call most strongly to me, were Maryland's complex Album Quilts, rather than West Virginia's simpler Nine Patches.

Mid-19th-century Album Quilts today seem born again as metaphor, evoking American history (Westward expansion, war, peace, commerce, monumental architecture, Friendly Benefit Societies, fraternal orders, the Great Awakening, Methodism, Odd Fellowdom, temperance, abolition, women's rights, admission of new states into the Union, Baltimore's role in the War of 1812, the Mexican American War, revolutions in transportation, industry, economics, even in political parties); the Language of Flowers, the Cult of Piety, the Cult of Domesticity, the Cult of Beauty, fancywork; the heyday of Natural History, the Audubon Era, the Age of Exhibitions; the emergence of Lady Bountiful, of American volunteerism and charitable activities; women's friendships, women's work, and above all, women as piecers, stitchers, connectors, quiltmakers. Through Album Quilts, we see quiltmaking as a supremely expressive art and as a refined craft. Now, late in the 20th century, quilting has also merged into a powerful figure of our national speech. Clearly, though it surprises quiltmakers not at all, quiltmaking has "arrived."

The history of the mid-19th-century Album Quilts must be a patchwork history, piecing together scraps of irregular form and disparate origin. Thus made whole, Album Quilts form a remarkable aspect of material culture, one whose breadth is not yet fully apparent nor even fully comprehensible. As with any metaphor, there is a tension between the Album's physical reality, which we actually see, and the vision of our mind's eye. These quilts blanket a mysterious union of that which we know objectively, merging with all that our experience, research, and imagination lead us to believe subjectively. Significantly the Album Quilt metaphor is composed of appliquéd cloth—collected on a theme and often embellished with both ink and embroidery—patched together, then layered with batting, backed, quilted through and through, then bound. This construction is appropriately complex: Our understanding of what these antebellum quilts tell us about their makers and ourselves, rides on the Album Quilt's magic carpet, not on the Nine Patch's homey simplicity.

Beginning with *Spoken Without a Word* (1983) and continuing through this ninth book on the subject, I've examined the patches of history and culture reflected in vintage Baltimore-style Album Quilts. Happily, both the historic bedrock and my own intuitions recounted in those earlier works, seem still to ring true. Yet substantial questions remain. Like squares to be integrated into an Album, questions still lie on the table. For example: What was the mechanism of popularization for the Baltimore Album Quilts? What was this style's conduit for transmission? What goals or constraints framed the production of so many of these quilts within a relatively short time period? Why, too, does this challenging vintage style call so strongly to quiltmakers today that, inheritors of the sewing machine though they are, they devote endless hours to hand-stitching Revivalist Baltimore Albums? To what degree can present Album Quiltmaking illuminate the past?

As though to fête C&T's 1994 Baltimore Album Revival Show and Contest, recent new discoveries have dramatically increased our understanding of Baltimore's old Albums. On the 10th anniversary of *Spoken Without a Word* in 1993, I went down to the Library of Congress to ferret out a fragmentary clue about quilts hung at "Maryland fairs." Intrigued, I had tried to pick up on this snatch of conversation from a researcher who had phoned to consult me about Baltimore's Albums. Impatient for lack of response to my query letter, I was trying my luck in the library's musty card catalog archives. Serendipitously—like a celebratory gift from the past—critical documents rewarded my search. These unearthed "Maryland Institute for the Promotion of the Mechanic Arts" catalogs, pamphlets, and broadsides paint a much clearer picture of who made the classic Albums. Among them are the Judges' Catalogs, which list by name the Album makers whose quilts were hung, beginning in 1848, at the annual Baltimore Mechanic Institute exhibitions.

My article "Albums, Artizans, and Odd Fellows" (*Folk Art Magazine,* Spring 1994) reflects this recent research and answers many of those questions raised above. Promised here in *Volume III,* but too lengthy in its final form to include, it has lead to this book's sequel, *Stitched in Cloth, Carved in Stone.* Among that book's multiple Album topics, the role of both the Mechanic Arts Movement (also known as the Mechanic Charitable Institutes) and the Age of Exhibitions in American Quiltmaking are explored. Concerning contemporary Album makers, the 1994 show catalog, *Baltimore Album Revival! Historic Quilts in the Making,* takes a timely look at why we today may find Albums so compelling. There, too, in a remarkable echo of Baltimore's antebellum Album era, are cataloged the cream of contemporary Album Quilts.

For late-20th-century quiltmakers, the Albums have been a treasure trove of appliqué technique and design inspiration. Indeed, the Album Quilts have been benefactresses of fabled generosity, so much have we learned from them. All across the quilt world, one can see old Baltimore's gifts: They are there in dimensional appliqué, in a plethora of finer appliqué, and in a renewed interest in symbolism. For those of us who began our Album Quiltmaking quest in *Volume I,* 12 lessons surveyed the types of appliqué witnessed by the Album blocks. The first half-dozen how-to lessons of *Volume I* teach variations on "cut-away," "one-layer," or "whole cloth" appliqué. Of all the ways to appliqué, and to design for appliquéd Albums, these "papercuts" have long been my favorites. These "best" have been saved for this volume.

Not surprisingly, while I was bent upon saving the best for close-to-last, our collective appliqué skills grew just as our appliqué design loves broadened. A fascination with Baltimore's floral fabric manipulations trained our eye to see a similar artistry reflected in her offerings of fruit. Those techniques, too, have been explored in this volume. But Papercut Appliqué still seems a perfect note on which to crescendo this series. Since childhood, papercuts were my first art/craft love and the cut-away method began me on hand appliqué to the exclusion, for a while, of all other forms of quiltmaking. In some ways, Papercut Albums are the easiest but also the most expressive Album Quilts. Their appliqué is soothingly straightforward, their block design almost formula-easy, and their setting together is aided by the simplicity of the blocks' palette, design, and construction. The Color Sections spotlight magnificent contemporary Papercut Album Quilts. The link to antebellum Baltimore is supplied by Quilt #6, Classic Revival: Alex's Album, inspired by Baltimore's Seidenstricker Album. "1845" is appliquéd upon that older quilt's border, and its picture is in both W. R. Dunton's *Old Quilts* and in the Baltimore Museum of Art's 1982 show catalog. Quilt #7, Friendship's Offering, is also closely based on an antique Album, a red-and-green one made by Sarah Holcombe and inscribed "1847" and "Lancaster." A picture of that original quilt is in Robert Bishop's *New Discoveries in American Quilts,* page 84 (listed in *Volume I's* bibliography).

Like a fireworks finale—brighter, louder, bigger—this book's Pattern Section is unparalleled in the number of its offerings: There are 85 Album block patterns. All manner of Album Quilt patterns are included. There are lush fruit block patterns and innovative lessons on how to add dimension, shading, and contour to these offerings of plenty. But by far the greatest number of patterns are for the Papercut Albums. These blocks can, in the fashion of Baltimore, be mixed with other Album blocks. The temptation may be irresistible, though, to mix pre-patterned papercut blocks with significant patterns of your own design. If you do set out to make a Papercut Album, *Design a Baltimore Album Quilt* offers a simple design method for working out your quilt's set. Beginning in *Volume II,* continuing in *Dimensional Appliqué,* and culminating in *Appliqué 12 Borders and Medallions!* the *Baltimore Beauties* series provides you with dozens of border patterns with which to frame your quilt.

In addition to papercuts and plenty, history and how-to, *Volume III* includes brief biographies of those modern women whose needlework it boasts. For those who stitch Baltimore-style in shop or friendship groups, there are exciting, challenging new classes, drawing both on this book and on previous books. And for those of you who have not yet heard the news, C&T's 1998 Baltimore Album Quilt Show, Contest, and Call for Honored Teachers is also previewed. Finally, there is a quite wonderful gift to all of us from my editor, Louise Townsend: She has carefully researched and here includes a nine-book index of the *Baltimore Beauties* series! Thus, if basket patterns for a Baltimore Basket Album are your need, or one-layer blocks for a Papercut Album, or you seek fruit block patterns to inspire a wreathed Della Robbia center medallion, now we have a carefully researched index right here at our fingertips.

Having had this introduction, please enjoy all that this book offers. No basic Nine Patches are to be found herein, but the techniques offered are simply taught and quickly mastered. For your efforts, you'll join so many others who have found Album Quiltmaking a comforting, challenging, and fulfilling heirloom art form. Perhaps you've come on our visit to Baltimore and Beyond, just for the company. Or perhaps you're intent upon finishing an Album already begun. Perhaps this volume is your very first introduction to the Baltimore Album style. Whatever the reason, thank you for joining me here in *Volume III,* on this journey to Baltimore and Beyond. Your presence and enthusiasm gives me such pleasure, and I so appreciate your company!

*Elly Sienkiewicz*
*January 6, 1994*
*Washington, D.C.*

# HOW TO USE THIS BOOK

Revivalist Baltimore quiltmakers are in communion. We sense that the happiness of making an Album Quilt is "in the journey, not at the end of the road." For some, there was a spectacular pause in the journey to display finished masterpieces at C&T Publishing's 1994 Baltimore Album Revival! Contest and Show in Lancaster, Pennsylvania. Even with their quilt-show submissions, though, so many entrants noted a continuing Album quest and avowed sights still fixed firmly on yet another heirloom star. Feeling, then, "as with those who journey together," the assumption here is that you have already read *Baltimore Beauties and Beyond, Volume I* of this series and have it nearby as a reference. Thus little from that volume is repeated here.

If, however, you have not yet read *Volume I*—or have never mastered cut-away or freezer paper appliqué—consider doing so now, for *Volume I* will teach you precisely how to translate these *Volume III* appliqué designs into cloth. From essential skills like turning points, curves, and corners, to appliqué uses of freezer paper and other modern materials, *Volume I* is the perfect how-to companion to this book's appliqué design lessons. *Papercuts and Plenty, Volume III of Baltimore Beauties and Beyond, Studies in Classic Album Quilt Appliqué,* presents four stitchery and design lessons, each with a wealth of techniques, and 85 block patterns. In addition, seven Album Class curriculums

and an index to the patterns, quiltmakers, and techniques in the *Baltimore Beauties* series are given.

Pattern notes for the block patterns refer to how-to-appliqué lessons from *Volume I* and give pertinent background information. Full-color photos of the pattern blocks will help you select your appliqué fabric. "Part One: Getting Started" in *Volume I* provides important information on how to transfer patterns from the book to make your own finished-size pattern, 12½" square. You'll also want to refer to *Volume II* and *Design a Baltimore Album Quilt!* Between them, these give 17 full border patterns, divulge the secrets of the classic Album sets, and interpret their quilting and binding. A full dozen more Album border and central medallion patterns fill *Appliqué 12 Borders and Medallions!*

Glorious quilts, both antique and modern, are exhibited in this volume. Throughout this book, when a quilt is referred to by number (as Quilt #2, or Quilt #7), you will find it pictured in the Color Section. If you'd like to meet the needleartists who worked on the contemporary quilts and blocks pictured, see "Part Three: The Quiltmakers." When a specific block is referred to, for example, as "Quilt #4, block D-3," that block can be located by its letter and number: The letters refer to the block position in the quilt, reading from left to right, and the numbers refer to position from top to bottom.

# PART ONE:
# THE PLEASURES OF PLENTY
## EXTOLLING THE FRUITS OF THE EARTH

# LESSON 1

## DIMENSIONAL FRUIT IN BOWLS, EPERGNES, AND HORNS OF PLENTY

### PATTERN:
"Epergne of Fruit IV," Pattern #85

The fruit bowl has a homey familiarity. A mesh bag of oranges, once pulled from the grocery sack, is torn, then emptied into the appointed bowl. Were there not something of reverence about the task, the refrigerator bin would be a more practical container. My large majolica fruit bowl—sided with cabbage-green ceramic leaves—belonged to my grandmother. It came to me mended by my mother, its flat bottom a matrix of shards epoxied back together. Empty, it looks like a reconstructed archaeological artifact. It looks revered. And for me it is a sort of family relic. I try to keep it filled with each season's harvest. It pleases me to set out velvety peaches, wine-dark apples, burnished pears—all verses of "This is the day, which the Lord hath made. Let us rejoice and be glad in it."

How will my grandmother's few remaining goods divide up when I'm gone? How to give each child a tangible reminder of Nana's part in what has made us what we are? But then, the answer comes: What a fine resting place for a family's fruit bowl an Album square would be! And what a pleasant way to eke one well-worn bowl, beautifully into three.

Admiringly, the classic Baltimores offer up an abundance of fruitful plenty, in praise. Yet few of us have seen close-up, the delightful techniques and clever realism with which this fruit was rendered. Having determined to learn even these secrets, we've now gone on to add our own unique touches to these portraits of plenty. Thus, both the old ways unearthed and the new ways discovered, are taught in these lessons. Reproducing the pedestaled bowl, "Epergne of Fruit IV," is a fine place to start: Though relatively simple, it will delight us with some quite glorious techniques. In these lessons, we'll call it "Wendy's Fruit Bowl," named for Wendy Grande, my talented assistant at California's Asilomar Quilt Conference who pioneered its making. The prototype for Wendy's bowl is a surprisingly dimensional block in a Numsen Family Baltimore Album pictured in *Stitched in Cloth, Carved in Stone*.

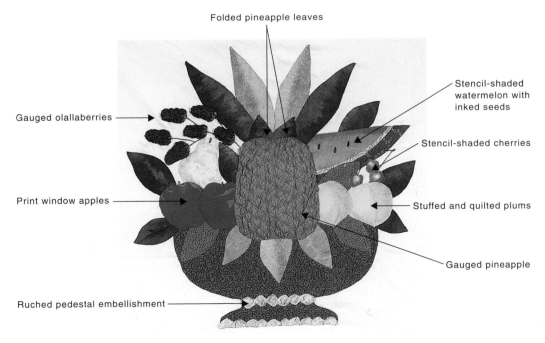

FIGURE 1-1  In these lessons, we'll call this charming design Wendy's Fruit Bowl. Its official title is *Epergne of Fruit IV*, and it is Pattern #85 in the Pattern Section.

# SPEED YOUR PATTERN TRANSFER

### Method 1: Transfer by Tracing

You can take a papercut pattern (Patterns #1-69 in the Pattern Section) from this book by drawing. As detailed on page 22 in *Volume I's* "Getting Started," you do this by folding a 12½" square of freezer paper into eighths, then trace the ⅛th pattern onto one corresponding eighth of the folded freezer paper. Staple within the appliqué motif to prevent shifting, and cut the "snowflake" out through all eight layers. Remove the staples and unfold the full pattern.

After folding the 12½" Freezer Paper Transfer Square into quarters, open it flat. Then glue the four photocopied pattern quadrants to its non-shiny side.

### Method 2: Transfer by Photocopying

You can take a layered pattern (Patterns #70-85 in the Pattern Section) from this book most quickly by photocopying.

First, photocopy the four pages for Pattern #85, for example. Then, cut out each page's pattern quadrant. Using spray adhesive, glue each quadrant onto it's quarter of the folded 12½" freezer paper square. Congratulations! You've now gotten the whole pattern onto the freezer paper without having had to trace it.

The next step is: Working on a light box, trace the pattern (tracing ⅛" inside each motif's outline) onto the right side of your fabric square. When this is done, go on to the third step: As you need a freezer paper template for any appliqué shape on the block, simply cut the freezer paper pattern apart. A warning, though: If you use *Volume I's* Freezer Paper on Top method of appliqué, use a press cloth to protect your iron from the photocopy's carbon. If you use the Freezer Paper Inside method, proceed as usual.

## MARKING THE BACKGROUND FABRIC

Using a light box, draw Pattern #85 onto the right side of the background cloth. To orient the pattern, fold the background square into quarters and finger-press the fold lines. Pin a photocopy or tracing of the pattern beneath the cloth square, matching cloth creases to the vertical and horizontal center lines of the pattern itself. If your cloth is not sufficiently opaque to see through, work on a light box. Trace the pattern onto the right side of the cloth with a lead pencil or a Pigma® .01 pen in brown, and iron to heat-set it. What do you mark on the cloth? Mark the shapes of each element of the pattern—fruit, leaves, bowl—but reduce their size slightly so that you are marking a good ⅛" inside the pattern's actual printed outline. This is critical. Such "reduced-shape marking" is easily read for placement. But because the lines are drawn inside the sewn shape's outline, they are easily covered by it.

## APPROACHING THE APPLIQUÉ

*Volume III* has so many new techniques to share that the step-by-step approach to Wendy's Fruit Bowl will rest on what you learned in *Volume I*. It's useful, though, to think the block through before you begin. What method will you use to prepare your appliqués? The method always depends on what you are sewing and on your preferences. Because our lesson block's shapes are so streamlined and simple, I, myself, would use the "Freezer Paper Inside" method from pages 77-78 in *Volume I*. Before you do any sewing however, read through these lessons in Part One. Then, just before sewing, lay the prepared shapes out on the marked background cloth to doublecheck your fabric selection and color choices. Next, consider the layering required. Which patch overlaps another? Anything that appears to lie underneath something else has to be sewn down first. All this points to our fulsome fruit bowl as the ideal place to start the final appliqué. But first, before you even choose your

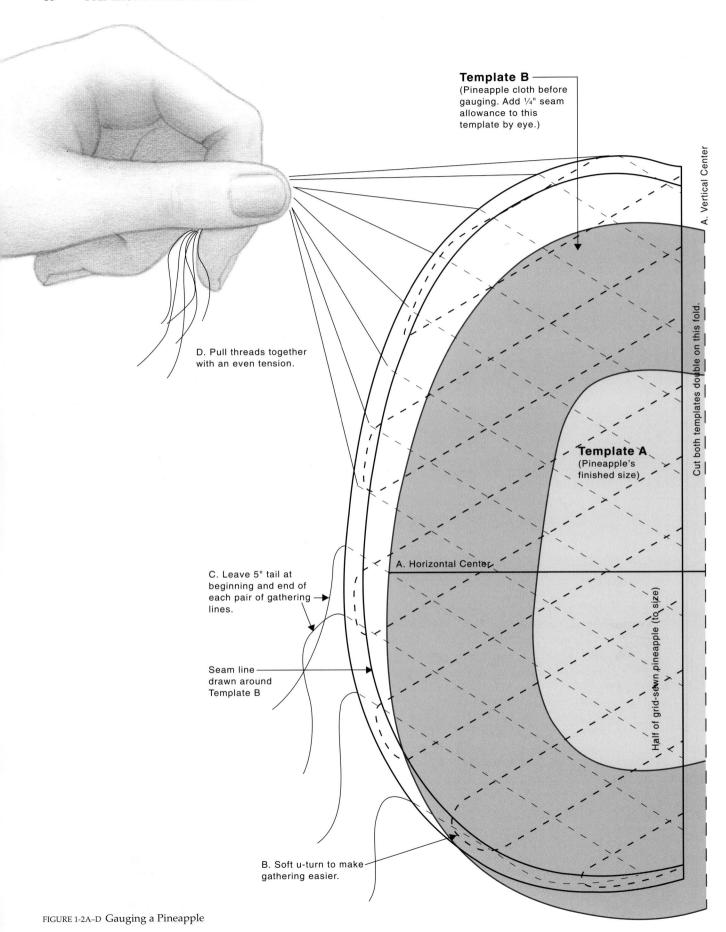

**Template B**
(Pineapple cloth before gauging. Add ¼" seam allowance to this template by eye.)

A. Vertical Center

Cut both templates double on this fold.

D. Pull threads together with an even tension.

**Template A**
(Pineapple's finished size)

Half of grid-sewn pineapple (to size)

C. Leave 5" tail at beginning and end of each pair of gathering lines.

A. Horizontal Center

Seam line drawn around Template B

B. Soft u-turn to make gathering easier.

FIGURE 1-2A–D Gauging a Pineapple

fabric, look over these lessons. They present novel methods for creating actual dimension or the semblance of dimension in various fruits. Having given yourself this overview, you can then approach this charming block by your own path.

## GAUGING IN NEEDLEWORK

Gauging is a patterned gathering whereby a larger shape is made to fit into a smaller area. The term comes from "gauge" meaning "to bring to correct gauge. To conform to a standard." It is an old art needlework technique used to texture cloth. It is also a dressmaking technique where, for instance, it could reduce the wrist cuff in a sleeve's voluminous fullness. When the gathering is done in a diagonal grid pattern, gauging echoes a pineapple's diamond-latticed surface with a splendid realism. Our inspiration for a gauged pineapple comes from this block's prototype in the antique Numsen quilt. Wendy Grande retraced the method in her dynamic version of that block, and so can you. If you like gauging's dimensional effect, try a tic-tac-toe grid on the olallaberries (Figure 1-3 on page 22) or gauge a cantaloupe with a curved line wedge (Figure 1-4 on page 23). To gauge the pineapple follow these steps, guided by Figure 1-2:

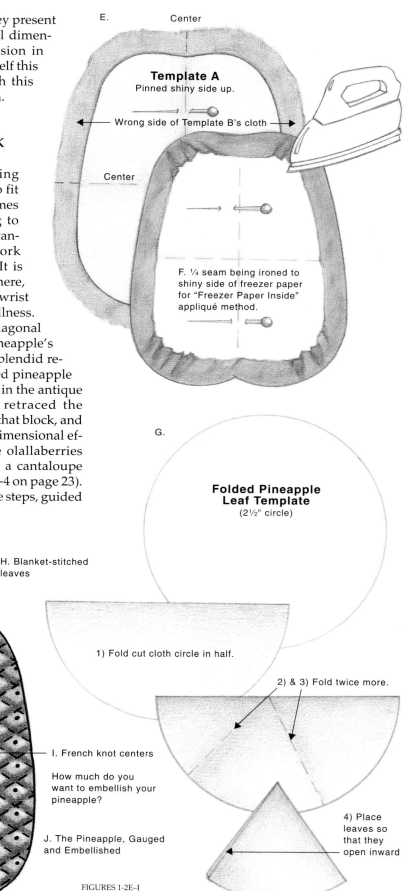

E.    Center

**Template A**
Pinned shiny side up.

← Wrong side of Template B's cloth →

Center

F. ¼ seam being ironed to shiny side of freezer paper for "Freezer Paper Inside" appliqué method.

G.

**Folded Pineapple Leaf Template**
(2½" circle)

1) Fold cut cloth circle in half.

2) & 3) Fold twice more.

4) Place leaves so that they open inward

H. Blanket-stitched leaves

I. French knot centers

How much do you want to embellish your pineapple?

J. The Pineapple, Gauged and Embellished

FIGURES 1-2E–J
Gauging a Pineapple, continued

## PREPARATION FOR GAUGING

1.  Cut Pineapple Template A (the pineapple's finished size) out of freezer paper. Cut it double on the fold and add no seam allowance.

2.  Cut Pineapple Template B out of freezer paper, double on the fold, adding no seam allowance. Template B is the cloth shape you will gather to the pineapple's finished size.

3.  Draw Template B on the right side of the pineapple's cloth, then add a $\frac{1}{4}$" seam allowance as you cut this shape out. By gauging (that is, shirring or gathering), this shape will be reduced to half its size, making it equivalent in size to Template A.

4.  Finger-press creases to mark the vertical and horizontal center of the cut cloth version of Template B (Figure 1-2A). Finger-press these same registration marks in Template A.

5.  Marking the diamond grid: Photocopy Figure 1-2. Use it as a guide to transfer Template B's diamond-grid to the cut cloth. To draw the grid on the cloth, use a light box, a gridded ruler to keep your lines parallel, and a mechanical pencil. (Or use dressmaker's carbon, a gridded ruler, and a ballpoint pen.) Extend the template's lines to cover the right side of the pineapple cloth. Lightly penciled, the grid-lines should not be noticeable after the cloth is gathered. If the marking is intrusive, simply mark the wrong side of the cloth instead.

6.  Next, draw a connection in the seam allowance between each pair of two lines that run from upper right to lower left (Figure 1-2B). Then connect each set of lines running from upper left to lower right. (*Hint from Wendy Grande:* When you stitch this connection, stitch it as a soft U-turn to make the gathering easier.)

## GAUGING A PINEAPPLE

1.  To hand-gather the pineapple's penciled grid, thread a quilting needle with 18" of strong quilting or sewing thread in a color matched to the cloth. Don't knot the thread.

2.  Leave a 5" tail to begin running stitches down the uppermost drawn line of a pair of lines that run from upper left to lower right (Figure 1-2C). Leave a 5" tail when you reach the top of this pair's second line. (All the grid lines, then, will have 5" tails when you've finished the gathering stitches.) Make fine running stitches to make fine shirring.

3.  After all the upper-left-to-lower-right lines have been stitched, sew the same gathering stitches along the upper-right-to-lower-left lines. At intersections, take care not to put your needle through any of the previous line's stitches. Doing so would stop the thread from gathering when you pull it. (*Machine Gauging Hint:* If you choose to machine-sew your gauging straight stitches, put one color thread in the bobbin for all the lines traveling in one direction, then change the bobbin thread color for those going in the opposite direction. When necessary to avoid stitching through previous sewing, lift the presser foot and push the fabric backward slightly. To gather, pull first one color bobbin thread, then the other. —from Candace Kling in *Threads,* August/September 1987, page 61.)

4.  To gather, hold the cloth in one hand, and pull all the thread ends aimed in one direction with the other hand. If pulling all the threads at once seems too much to handle on a shape of this size, pull the pineapple's top half threads first (Figure 1-2D). Next pull the bottom half. Pull all the threads with the same tension. Pull until the shirred folds are a fat quarter inch apart (Figure 1-2J) or half the size of the original grid.

5.  Repeat Step 4 to gather the threads running in the opposite direction. When finished, you should have a cloth gathered to the size of Template A, but with an additional $\frac{1}{4}$" seam allowance around it. If there is, in fact, a $\frac{1}{4}$" seam allowance outlining Tem-

plate A (Figure 1-2E), you are brilliant! If the seam allowance is off-size, you are nonetheless wonderful, but will need to adjust the gathers to size. When to-size, tie off the paired threads to hold the gathers and cut off their tails.

6.  Pin Template A's freezer paper pattern—shiny side up—to the wrong side of the gauged fabric, matching both vertical and horizontal center creases (Figure 1-2E, also).

7.  Using a dry, hot (linen setting) iron and a hard surface, iron the ¼" seam smoothly down to the paper's edge (Figure 1-2F). The plastic will meld to the seam and hold it in place for sewing.

8.  Appliqué the underlying foliage, then the pineapple and its own leaves to the foundation square. To remove the pineapple's freezer paper template, go to the block's wrong side and, behind the appliqué, make a 1½" bias slit in the background cloth. With tweezers, pull the freezer paper template out through this opening. There's no need to mend the cut.

## DIMENSIONAL PINEAPPLE LEAVES

Even shopping at urban East Coast grocery stores, I sometime learned to pluck out a central pineapple leaf, and by the ease with which it detached, so test the fruit's ripeness. (Green-picking and cold storage have made sniffing for ripeness almost obsolete in our local produce sections!) The tight concentric nestling of the pineapple's leaves, their deep green sturdiness, their fibrous sharpness are familiar; so we all enjoy a good caricature of these aspects in appliqué. When I saw dimensional folded foliage (Figure 1-2G) on an Album Pineapple, it reminded me of those stiff, nesting leaves and brought a smile of recognition to my thoughts. Then on Sue Linker's Pineapple (Color Plate #6), I spotted serrate leaf edges imitated by spiky blanket stitching (its legs marching stiffly around the leaf and over the background cloth), and I knew I was seeing another Album "touch of genius"! (Figure 1-2H)

To make dimensional folded pineapple leaves, cut a 2½" diameter circle of green and fold it (right sides out) according to Figure 1-2G. The circle is folded in half, then this semi-circle's sides are folded (not quite in thirds) in towards the center. Place the leaves so that the open side of both leaves face each other. Ease the fullness at the leaves' bases as you appliqué the pineapple over their raw edges.

## EMBELLISHING THE PINEAPPLE

For a finishing touch, use two strands of yellow sewing thread to sew a french knot in the center of each of the pineapple's surface squares. The french knot is illustrated by Figure 1-6 on page 25. If you'd like to blanket-stitch the leaves, there is a fine drawing of how to do the blanket stitch in *Dimensional Appliqué*, page 56. On the leaves, sewing thread (two strands) or a single strand of embroidery floss or quilting thread is suggested. Simply sew the stitches' legs facing away from the appliqué, but pointing on a diagonal, towards the outer leaf-tip.

## WENDY GRANDE'S GAUGED OLALLABERRIES

Imagine other fruit or vegetables, which, gauged, could add dimensional appliqué's zest, as well as a touch of realism to your Album block. Maize—a cob of corn—for instance, could be gauged to a kerneled texture. For corn, the grid sewn would be a tic-tac-toe grid. This is the same grid we'll use here for succulent berries. Osage oranges or "ugly fruit," on the other hand, could be gauged with meandering—rather than straight—gathering lines. Wendy Grande included plump olallaberries (Figure 1-3A) from home in her family's fruit bowl. Cut Template A in freezer paper for the finished berry size. Use Template B (page 22) to draw the berry's pre-gathered cloth shape on the right side of the cloth, adding a ¼" seam when you cut it.

To make the olallaberries, follow the directions for Preparation for Gauging for the pineapple. Mark Template B on the right side of the cloth with a grid of lines ¼" apart, set at right angles to each other (Figure 1-3B). Guided by the Gauging the Pineapple instructions, Steps 1-5, leave 3" tails, stitch, and pull the threads to gather the grid lines (Figure 1-3C). Then follow Steps 6-8. Prepare the appliqué by ironing the seam down to freezer paper Template A, the olallaberry's finished size.

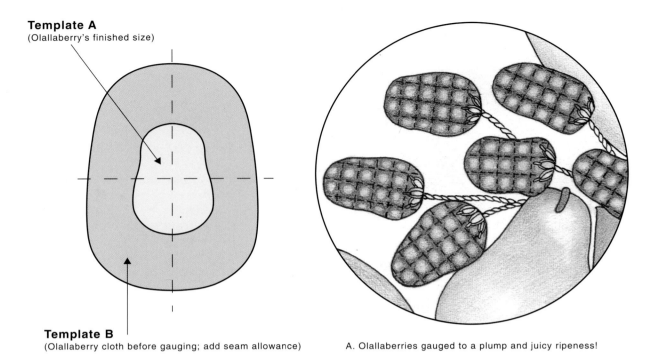

**Template A**
(Olallaberry's finished size)

**Template B**
(Olallaberry cloth before gauging; add seam allowance)

A. Olallaberries gauged to a plump and juicy ripeness!

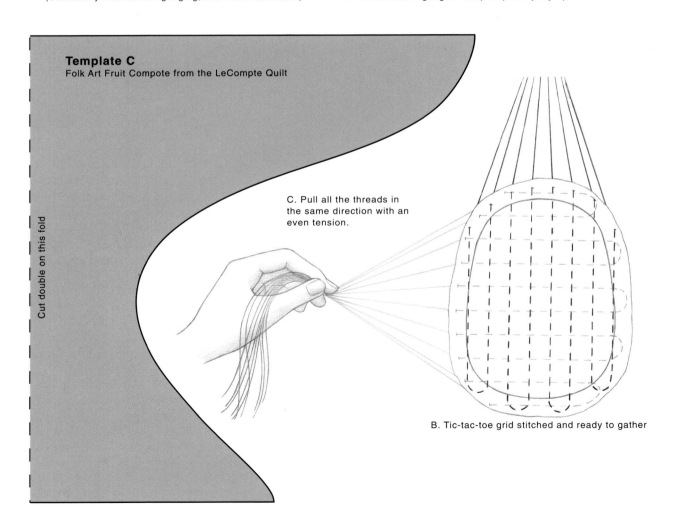

**Template C**
Folk Art Fruit Compote from the LeCompte Quilt

Cut double on this fold

C. Pull all the threads in the same direction with an even tension.

B. Tic-tac-toe grid stitched and ready to gather

FIGURE 1-3 A–C  Gauging Olallaberries (Plus a Folk Art Fruit Compote Template)

## GAUGING A MARYLAND CANTALOUPE OR MUSKMELON

Maryland grows heavenly cantaloupes! A magnificently dimensional cantaloupe is pictured in a block from the antique LeCompte Family Album on page 56, in *Volume I.* While not in Wendy's Fruit Bowl, we'll observe here how a cantaloupe (Figure 1-4) could be made because it teaches us that gauging can be done not just with grids, but also with the lines running all in one direction. To inspire a fruit block with cantaloupe, the LeCompte block's folk art compote is Figure 1-3's Template C. These next steps show how to gauge a cantaloupe:

1.  Cut the cantaloupe's Template A out of freezer paper, adding no seam allowance.

2.  Draw Template B on the cantaloupe cloth's right side. Add a ¼" seam allowance as you cut out this shape.

3.  Using a light box or dressmaker's carbon paper, draw Template B's gathering lines on the right side of the cantaloupe cloth shape.

4.  There are three pairs of gathering stitch lines: These are gathering lines A (on the cantaloupe's outside edges), gathering lines B (at right and left sides), and gathering lines C near its center. Leave a 4" tail at the beginning and end of running stitches taken along each pair of lines (Figure 1-4C).

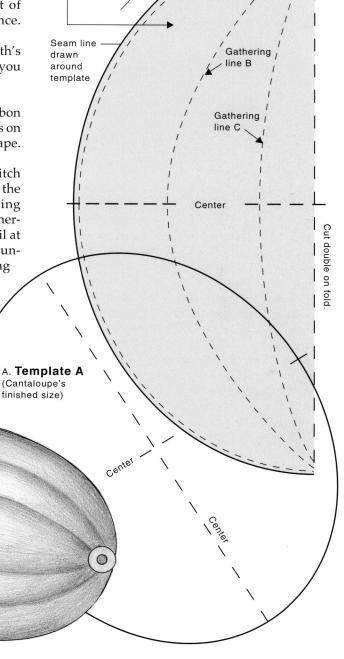

B. **Template B**
(Cantaloupe cloth, before gauging. Add ¼" seam allowance along edge.)

C.

Gathering line A

Seam line drawn around template

Gathering line B

Gathering line C

Center

Cut double on fold.

A. **Template A**
(Cantaloupe's finished size)

Center

Center

D. Finished cantaloupe

FIGURE 1-4A–D  Gauging a Maryland Cantaloupe or Muskmelon

5.  Pull all the threads at once, to gather, keeping the tension even. By this gauging, reduce the shape about one third in size. You're finished when the shirred cloth shape is just ¼" bigger all around than the cantaloupe's freezer paper Template A. Secure, then trim, the threads.

6.  Complete the appliqué (Figure 1-4D) as in the Pineapple's Steps 6-8 on page 21.

7.  To pad the cantaloupe's wedges: With thread matching the appliqué, take tiny top stitches along the gathered lines' length. (Top-stitching goes through the appliqué and into the background cloth.) From the wrong side of the background cloth, make one or two small slits within the stitched wedges. Using a fine crochet hook, push fiberfill into each wedge, stuffing until the appliqué resembles the scalloped circumference of a cantaloupe.

## BERRIES AS FRUIT ARRANGEMENT "FILLERS"

Sprays of berries make wonderful fillers for fruit still lifes. They serve much the same purpose that fern or baby's breath does in floral arrangements. Not only must such a filler visually soften the space between larger fruit, but (like fern and baby's breath) it is most useful when it costs little—in time and effort. Find a favorite filler in some of the simpler berries that follow or in others familiar to you. With its showy leaves, the strawberry, for example, frequents Album blocks. Why not embellish its surface with seed stitch in off-white? (See Figure 1-8). Then, too, there is the beloved Album stand-by, the currant or grape. It is taught both flat and filled, in *Volume I's* Lesson 9. Old engravings from Owen Jones's 1856 reference book, *The Grammar of Ornament*, are included on page 28 to give you the gesture of more berries and branches. Perhaps you'll find a place for your own interpretation of some of these amidst your Album's plenty.

## JEANNIE AUSTIN'S BLACKBERRIES

When, in an Album picture block, Jeannie Austin portrayed her childhood farm, she appliquéd into it summer's juiciest blackberries. Rather than use a straight or

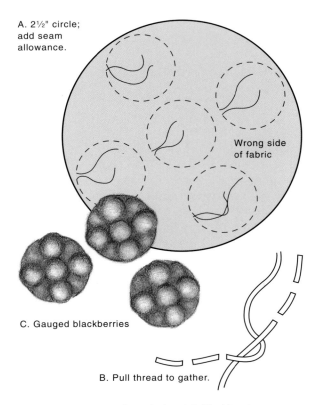

A. 2½" circle; add seam allowance.

Wrong side of fabric

C. Gauged blackberries

B. Pull thread to gather.

FIGURE 1-5A–C Jeannie Austin's Blackberries

meandering line to gauge the cloth, she sewed circles for the plumply dimensional berries, in the following manner:

1.  Draw a 2½" circle on the right side of your blackberry cloth. (Jeannie used a subtle print with highlights.) As you cut this out, add ¼" seam allowance.

2.  On the circle's wrong side, mark five dime-sized circles, not touching each other (Figure 1-5A).

3.  Gather-stitch each circle, leaving on the wrong side, a 2½" thread tail where you begin and end that single circle (Figure 1-5A, also).

4.  Loop one thread end under the other (Figure 1-5B), then pull to gather the circle to about half its size. Knot the threads to secure the gathers.

5.  On the background cloth, draw a nickel-sized circle for each berry. Appliqué the berry down by turning under its ¼" seam. Pull the circle's drawn seam line into alignment, so that it covers the circle penciled on the background cloth beneath it (Figure 1-5C).

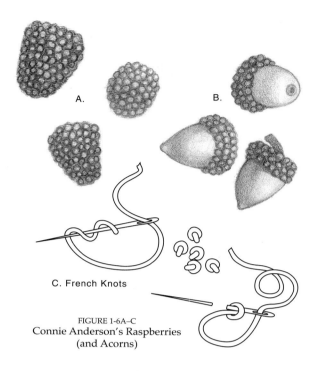

C. French Knots

FIGURE 1-6A–C
Connie Anderson's Raspberries
(and Acorns)

## CONNIE ANDERSON'S RASPBERRIES

Sunny Florida, one of our nation's most fertile fruit baskets, has produced inspired Album Quiltmaking as well. Connie Anderson does perfectly exquisite work and shares her talents through teaching. When I first held her blocks, I looked at them very slowly, so beautifully were they made. I came to a complete halt on "Eight-Pointed Star with Sprigs of Berries" from *Spoken Without a Word*. She had rendered that pattern with exquisite attention to detail: Its berries were composed of dozens of tiny french knots, compactly stitched with a single strand of sewing thread (Figure 1-6C). The idea is brilliant—and versatile. Depending on the thread (sewing thread or hand embroidery thread) and the number of strands, one has quite a realm of possible berries at one's fingertips! Connie confined her french knots within the area of perfect circles. Simply by changing the shape, you could make french knot berries more raspberry-like (Figure 1-6A).

Album Quilt makers-of-old loved to tuck acorns and oak leaves in amongst their fruit. One understands that these symbolized admired attributes: Acorns mean longevity; the oak, strength in adversity. Figure 1-6B shows some french knot-capped acorns, while Figure 1-6C reminds you how a french knot is made. Both the symbolism of various fruit and a full-scale pattern for a diagonally-set cornucopia with acorns amidst its fruit, are in *Spoken Without A Word*.

## JEANNIE AUSTIN'S BLUEBERRIES

Jeannie's observation of nature is keen. The telling detail on her blueberries seems to reflect childhood's wonder at this small, sweet berry with its ruffled crown. Making this berry, one might remember the still heat of an August day broken only by the sawed song of grasshoppers; might recall the sweet perfume of hot grass, recently mowed. How long since you tried to wipe the cloudiness off a blueberry, like condensation off a window—but dreamy, not practical?

1.  On the right side of blueberry-colored fabric, trace the outline of a 25-cent piece. Cut a seam ⅛" outside the drawn line (Figure 1-7A).

2.  With a knotted thread color-matched to the cloth, straight-stitch on the drawn line. Leave your thread uncut (Figure 1-7B).

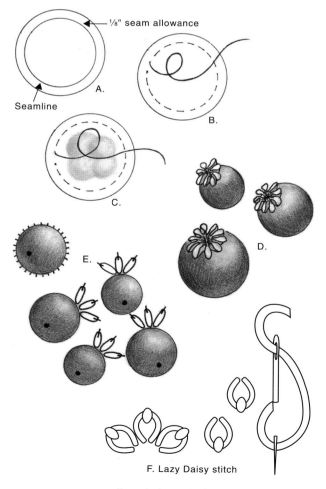

F. Lazy Daisy stitch

FIGURE 1-7A–F Jeannie Austin's Blueberries

3.   Put a scant ⅛th teaspoon pinch of fiberfill inside the sewn circle, on the cloth's wrong side (Figure 1-7C). (In a cluster of blueberries, you might want to stuff some, but not others, for the illusion of perspective.)

4.   Pull the thread, gathering the cloth as tightly as possible. Secure the thread (Figure 1-7D).

5.   Raw edges centered beneath the shape, blindstitch the berry to the background cloth (Figure 1-7E).

6.   Thread a crewel needle with one strand, 18" long and knotted, of moss green embroidery floss. Sew a french knot with just one twist of thread around its shank, below the berry's center. This french knot marks the base of the berry. Placing it as you have, just off-center and in the lower half of the fruit, adds a bit of perspective and hence, naturalism.

7.   Jeannie uses the same single strand of floss to loop three lazy daisy stitches at the top of the berry (Figure 1-7F).

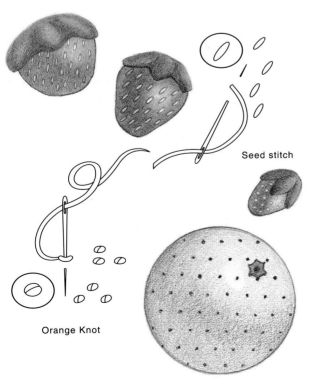

Seed stitch

Orange Knot

FIGURE 1-8  Summer Stawberries from an Old Album and
Minou Button's Dimpled Seville Oranges

*Option:* Step #4 leaves a raw-edged ruffle. Play with using it, trimmed, to form the berry's ruffled crown as in Figure 1-7D. Because the circle's edges are overwhelmingly bias-cut, this raw edge will not fray.

## MINOU BUTTON'S DIMPLED SEVILLE ORANGES

When I was 10, my mother cut a pattern for a yard-long Christmas stocking. I sewed and decorated three stockings from this pattern, for my older sister and younger brother and myself. Even just the foot itself was copious. Today, I wonder how a frugal mother could have designed it so. But Santa Claus had a clever formula: He filled the toe with citrus fruit, then added an imported marzipan bar, too. After those came serviceable packages of underwear—I was still getting nylons in my stocking when I married at age 27! Then an art tablet or two topped the stocking off. Whatever else went in probably cost more, but has long been forgotten. The simplest traditions, the most oft-repeated rituals, are what have lasted longest in memory.

As we worked on this project together, my mother told me that during her childhood in Cherbourg, France, an orange in the stocking toe was a coveted luxury: bright sweetness from sunny climes in winter's drear. I remembered a story-book illustration of oranges tucked into Dutch children's wooden shoes, confirming that fruit's worth on Christmas morning. For these and other reasons, oranges have always held romance for me. My grandmother long bought British marmalade in pottery jars, then taught me how to candy the fruit and make the marmalade itself. As a child, I used to wonder where warm-climate oranges for North Sea marmalade came from, adding mystery to romance amongst the wonders of an orange.

It seems quite fitting then, that when Gillian Clarke visited from England and showed pictures of friends' Album blocks, Minou Button's block contained a magnificent orange. Minou's touch of genius on this was a sprinkling of french knots in a diamond grid (Figure 1-8) over the orange's surface. The knots for her relatively small orange appear to have been tied in a single strand of sewing-weight thread, with one twist made round the needle's shank and the stitch pulled quite tightly. Her appliqué evokes all the dimpled magic of a tangy, juicy orange!

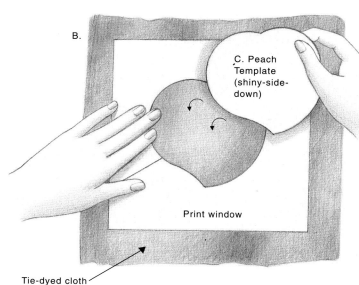

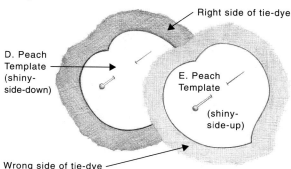

FIGURE 1-9A–F  A Plump and Quilted Greengage Plum or Peach

## A PLUMP AND QUILTED GREENGAGE PLUM OR PEACH

Unlike the fulsome roundness of an orange, a plum or peach has a shallow cleft between two rounded halves. This indentation is most easily evoked by padding the appliqué (Figure 1-9F) and quilting it to the background cloth. Using a "print window" (Figure 1-9A) to find the perfectly shaded spot in your cloth increases your fruit's realism even further. The charmingly varied colors of a blushing peach quite naturally invite using a print window with, say, tie-dyed fabric. So let's now review the print window technique (originally taught in *Dimensional Appliqué*, page 26) and investigate batting-quilted appliqué:

1.  Trace a peach from Pattern #85 onto a 3" square of freezer paper. Cut it out carefully, so that you have both the Peach Template (Figure 1-9A) and a Peach "Print Window" Template.

2.  Choose a tie-dye fabric or a large, splashy print, which has peach coloration possibilities in it. Move the print window over the cloth's right-side surface until a realistic-looking area is framed by the Peach Window Template (Figure 1-9B). Carefully place the Peach Template, shiny side down, over this patch of cloth (Figure 1-9C). It will be as though you are putting a jigsaw puzzle piece back into place. Place the template to capture that perfect patch of coloration framed by the print window.

3.  Trim a ¼" seam around the Peach Template (Figure 1-9D). Before removing the template, draw the seam line around it on the right side of the cloth. (If we were not going on to stuff and quilt this peach, we would switch the template to the wrong side of this trimmed fabric, then iron the seam to the shiny side of the template as in Figure 1-9E.)

4.  *Stuffing the Peach Appliqué.* We have three choices for stuffed appliqué. The first is to slit the background cloth and stuff it from the back. (This is how the

cantaloupe was stuffed.) The second is to leave an inch or so of the appliqué unsewn, slip in fiberfill from the side, then complete the appliqué. We'll use the third method here: Centered on the appliqué's wrong side, baste a piece of batting cut the same shape as the peach but ⅛" smaller all-around. (A sturdy felt-like batting works well. Warm and Natural™ is a good example of this.) Next baste (or pin) the batting-backed peach to the background cloth and appliqué it down by the needleturn method (*Volume I,* Lessons 1-2).

5.    Quilt (through to the background) the cleft in the peach, matching your thread to the peach's cloth color (Figure 1-9F, also).

Print windows were used throughout much of Wendy's Fruit Bowl (Pattern #85, Color Plate 2). They were used, for example, for the bright apples cut from a marbleized fabric, and to find the perfect section of cloth for other fruit and foliage. Another successful method for shading fruit to realistic dimension is to stencil your cloth, which we cover in Lesson 2.

# LESSON 2

## FABULOUS FRUIT— STENCILING TRICKS AND TECHNIQUES

**PATTERN:**
"Epergne of Fruit IV," Pattern #85

"Went to housekeeping." The phrase struck me. "This was the last quilt I made before I went to housekeeping," the quiltmaker, a Pennsylvanian in her 70s, had written to me in 1975, of a quilt sent on approval for purchase. The phrase set me to thinking about Albums. A century before Wal-Mart, it must have taken some years of putting-by to ready oneself for going to housekeeping. Perhaps the aspiration inspired a girl's youth as she made table and bed linens, looking to the future. (The way I'd worked toward getting into college: summer jobs, good grades, extra-curricular activities. The way I'd bought bits of china and glassware, and bargain basement negligees once in college—before I knew how uncomfortable nylon was, or how hemlines would make my

"hope chest" dowdy, long before I married.) The culture couched the necessity as virtue. "Keep within compass" was a mid-19th-century catch-phrase. Everyone knew that a woman's role encompassed caring, artful domesticity; knew that cultivating domesticity would help not only the family, but the very nation itself.

I think of how these convictions are reflected in the Albums and of how, in reproducing the Album style, we are passing on significant cultural threads that well predate even the mid-19th century. Take fruit, for example. The gravity-defying arrangements of fruit in epergnes seem clearly influenced by theorems. Even the word theorem is so old that its folk art usage is only hinted at in a modern dictionary: "from the Greek, 'to look at.'" The fruits themselves were part of the Victorian symbolic tongue, many of whose icons reach back into classic times. When we replicate a vintage Album's fruit block, we're passing on both the theorem painting, which preceded the Album period, and the even earlier art of stenciling. Stenciling was popular in 18th-century American craft. Shared stencil patterns could add a bit of color to decorate domestic woods and homemade furniture.

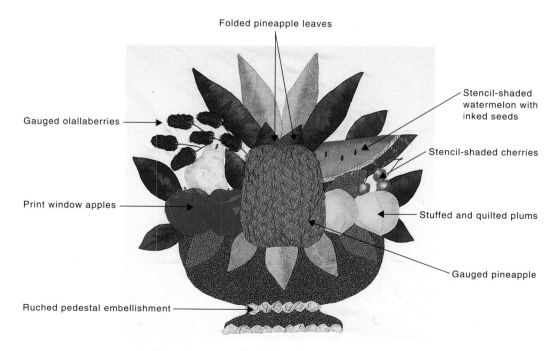

Folded pineapple leaves

Gauged olallaberries

Print window apples

Ruched pedestal embellishment

Stencil-shaded watermelon with inked seeds

Stencil-shaded cherries

Stuffed and quilted plums

Gauged pineapple

In these lessons, we'll call this charming design Wendy's Fruit Bowl. Its official title is *Epergne of Fruit IV*, and it is Pattern #85 in the Pattern Section.

# COLOR-BLENDING FOR REALISM

### Mixing Colors on the Palette

Perhaps you want the purpled blue of a damson plum. You can mix that color even before you stencil your appliqué. Simply wipe color from the blue paintstik onto your paper plate palette (Figure A). Next, wipe color from the purple paintstik over it. Blend the two together with the tip of your "fingermuslin" (Figure B). Test the color of the blend on a scrap of background cloth. Adjust the color, perhaps even adding red as a third element.

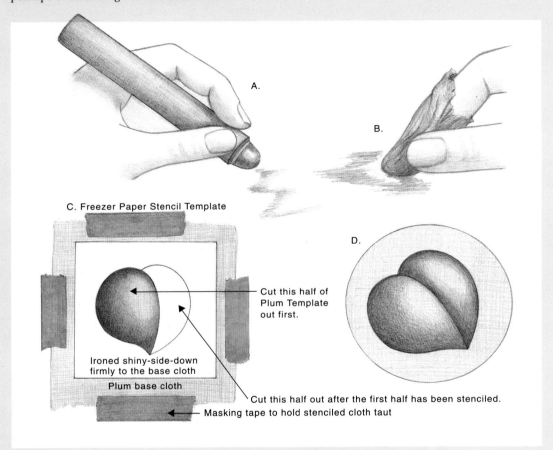

A.

B.

C. Freezer Paper Stencil Template

D.

Cut this half of Plum Template out first.

Ironed shiny-side-down firmly to the base cloth

Plum base cloth

Cut this half out after the first half has been stenciled.

Masking tape to hold stenciled cloth taut

### Mixing Colors on the Appliqué Cloth

A second way to blend colors is to stencil them consecutively onto the appliqué cloth so that the layers convey the desired tint and shade. For this to be successful, the paint must be applied in light, powdery layers. To avoid smearing the color:

• Remove any excess paint by daubing the fingermuslin off on a scrap of cloth before actually stenciling the appliqué.
• Allow a few minutes of drying time before applying the second layer.
• When the fruit has two rounded halves, shade them one at a time. To do this, cut open the larger stencil half (Figure C) and stencil it first. Then cut and stencil the smaller half. This gives a nice shadowed definition to the fruit's cleft.

To mix the damson plum's tints, apply the dominant blue color first. Use this to "sculpt" the plum, laying the blue paint down most thickly at the fruit's outside edge (Figure C). Taper the paint's density off as in Figure D, creating a highlight area where no stenciling has been done. This gives the fruit its three-dimensional quality and its basic color. Next, stencil the purple and then the red lightly over the blue to create the desired tint. After the base color has dried, a white highlight can be stenciled on top of it, though for appliqué, it seems best to let the background cloth create the shine.

Kate Fowle, a skilled contemporary stencil artist, taught me how to stencil fabric. I sought this technique both for Album Quilt realism and for the antique "rainbow" cloth's increasing saturations of tint that gave old Baltimore's Albums such painterly beauty. The shading process is made so easy by using freezer paper for the stencil and oil paint sticks for the color! There is no limit to what you can stencil in your appliqué block. You can stencil-shade over a print to give dimension to an urn, you can stencil on green to pep up a leaf, you can stencil berries directly onto the background cloth. Moreover, stenciling is so simple that just the following few examples should be enough to train your hand.

## SUPPLIES

- Paper towels for cleanup.

- A paper plate or thin cardboard to use either as a palette or to protect the working surface.

- A very hot-getting, dry iron to meld the freezer paper pattern stencil to the fruit's fabric. An old iron works well. The Black and Decker Classic® and the Bernina® iron are the best modern irons that I know of for use with the Freezer Paper on Top method.

- A hard surface to iron on, such as a breadboard or cardboard. A fabric bolt sleeve is ideal.

- Freezer paper (white, plastic-coated) for making stencil templates.

- Good 5" cut-to-the-point paper scissors for cutting stencils.

- Masking tape to adhere the to-be-stenciled cloth to the cardboard.

- A scrap of muslin (about 5" square) to wrap over your forefinger. This "finger muslin" serves as a stencil brush.

- Paint sticks (oil paint in solid stick form) are the best, most easy-to-use stencil paints I've found for this purpose. Laco Industries, Inc., makes Creative Art Products Paintstik® in handy boxed sets. Art supply stores and some quilt shops carry them. Read the instructions that come with the paints before starting.

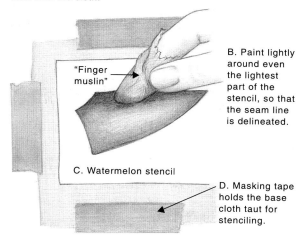

A. Push your finger muslin from the paper first, then onto the cloth.

"Finger muslin"

B. Paint lightly around even the lightest part of the stencil, so that the seam line is delineated.

C. Watermelon stencil

D. Masking tape holds the base cloth taut for stenciling.

FIGURE 1-10A–D Stenciling the Watermelon in Wendy's Fruit Bowl

## STENCILING THE WATERMELON IN WENDY'S FRUIT BOWL

### Preparation

1.  Cut a 4" x 6" swatch of your chosen appliqué cloth.

2.  Trace Pattern #85's watermelon flesh shape onto a rectangle of freezer paper. Cut the watermelon shape and remove it. The window left in the freezer paper rectangle becomes your stencil (Figure 1-10C).

3.  Use a dry, hot iron with the setting at "linen." Tightly iron the window template, shiny side down, to the right side of the watermelon fabric (Figure 1-10A). *Preview:* When you pull the paint across the stencil edge and onto the cloth, it will lay down color inward from the watermelon's outline. The outline becomes the most densely stenciled, thus also sharply defining the appliqué's seam line. Until the stenciling is complete, the fabric remains simply a "swatch," not yet cut to shape. Once stenciled, though, you'll trim the swatch back to ⅛" beyond the seam line in preparation for appliqué by the needleturn method.

4.  With masking tape, tape this swatch-with-stencil to your paper plate work surface (Figure 1-10D).

## FABRIC CHOICE FOR STENCILED FRUIT

The most obvious way for us to stencil fruit is to darken a lighter colored cloth. It makes sense, then, to choose light-hued base fabric for our stenciled appliqués. Sometimes a neutral is ideal. Kate Fowle used fine natural-colored muslin for her cherries in Figure B. Again, on the pears in Color Plate 7 she used a neutral, but this time a print, as the base cloth for stenciled pears. There, she cleverly imitated old Baltimore's patterned rainbow cloth, by stencil-shading a burnished bronze color over a decorative beige-on-white print (Figure A). In some instances, you may choose a medium tone fabric and stencil both the darker shadow and the lighter highlight onto it.

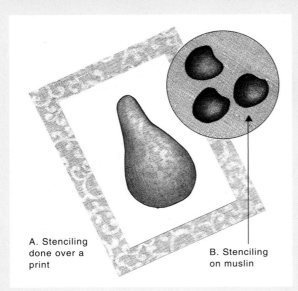

A. Stenciling done over a print

B. Stenciling on muslin

Surely one of old Baltimore's gifts has been to make us "stop and smell the flowers." Then, as we seek to stitch a particular blossom into our block, we need to find that flower, or to find its picture; to remember how its petals were mottled, or how its leaf was shaped. Sometimes for the first time really, we concentrate on the components that form such a beautiful whole. With an indefinable magic, this focus on botanical detail can make all cares slip away and fill our thoughts with wonder. As I write this, questions come to mind about how fruit appears. Are the highlights on different colored fruits always the same color as the fruit itself? Are they always white? Or are they simply a lighter shade of, say, an apple's classic red? Sometime in my childhood, I noted that the stem end of an orange carried a shape, which I've remembered as a star. Was it just imagination? I must go back and look. I'm told that in Japan, one brings fruit rather than flowers to one's hostess. Shapely, succulent, mythical fruit. The golden apples. The vineyard and its keeper. The family fruit bowl. Fruit reminds us of the human epic. Small wonder then, that the ladies of Baltimore stitched the fruits of the earth so lovingly into their quilts!

### Stenciling

Watermelon flesh ripens, sweetens, and darkens toward the melon's center. A lighter tone betokens a lessening of this lushness, the closer one gets to the rind. So for a watermelon, I might choose a light pink fabric and stencil red paint from the straight-cut inner edge toward the curved outer edge (Figure 1-10A). To lighten the color as you approach the curved edge, decrease the pressure to thin the layer of paint deposited. Lay the most paint along the straight-edge, right where you want the color darker (Figure 1-10A, also). Put some paint—even just a fine powder—on all the window's edges, to define the appliqué's seam line (Figure 1-10B). Alternatively, you could trace an unstenciled edge lightly with pencil to mark the seam line. To appliqué, cut a seam and needleturn

the melon's top edge under. The other edges will lie flat, covered by the neighboring pineapple, or hidden under the rind. Showing the watermelon's characteristic white rind just above the green skin is a touch of genius—inspired here not by old Baltimore, but by Jeannie Austin's contemporary block (Color Plate #1).

*Stenciling Goals:* Do a practice piece first and try to achieve a powdery, even layering, blotch-free. At its most skillful, stenciling will look washlike and as though it were integral to the fabric. Ideally, the observer will be a bit mystified as to how your remarkable realism has been achieved! Go back to *Baltimore Album Quilts, A Pattern Companion to Volume I,* and, beginning at the front cover block, study its close-up photographs. Many of them show the old "rainbow cloth" with

# PRINT WINDOWS, LIGHT SOURCES, AND INKED EMBELLISHMENTS

*Where is the Light Source?* We take our standard of stylized realism from the old Baltimores. When, in classes, we've worked together on fruits in baskets, compotes, and cornucopias, it's been fun to refine this tradition of realism. For example, if you mark the light source in the upper righthand corner of your layout pattern (Figure C), you'll know that the highlights face the light source's direction, the upper right; the most darkly shadowed side of each fruit faces the opposite direction, the lower left. We'll call this "solar-coding" and draw a sunny smile face to note the sun's position on our block. To keep the direction of the light source consistent, also mark the sun symbol on each fruit's freezer paper window template (Figures A and B). By two completely different techniques, this sun-emblazoned window template will help you keep the light/shadow side of your whole fruit offering realistically consistent. These techniques are:

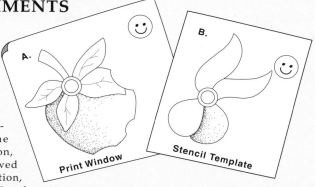

A. Print Window

B. Stencil Template

1. Use your solar-coded window template as a stencil to guide which side of the fruit you should darken with a powder of paint (Figure B).

2. Use your solar-coded window template as a print window, moving it over a shaded print to capture the perfectly positioned shadow (Figure A).

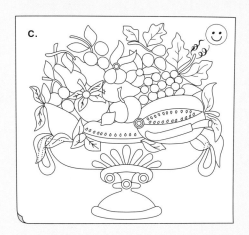

C.

*What is a Stem-well Circle?* At first I was mystified at the circled fruit centers. What was that "spot," that polka dot so often repeated? Then it dawned on me that what was intended was the shadowed valley around a stem—and further, that its inclusion on a fruit's simple shape was ingenious. To see what a difference a stem-well makes, hide a couple with your thumb (Figure C). The fruit will have lost an intriguing detail that both captures our interest and adds a touch of magic sparkle as well. What were these circles made out of, anyhow? Often, they were cut out of prints, and we see the same print used over and over in Album blocks. The printed circles were sometimes linked, sometimes solitary. Look at the cover of *Baltimore Album Quilts, A Pattern Companion to Volume I*. Find this circle print as the bird's claw, the bow's center, and as seeds and calyx on the flowers. In Color Plate 22, in the same book, you'll see a wonderful antique fruit cornucopia block, redolent with vintage rainbow prints and stem-well circles!

*Inking—the Finishing Touch:* Stems and leaves invite inking on both floral and fruit blocks. But fruit blocks also invite other inkings: First, there are those stem-wells, themselves, and watermelons seem always to have a row or two of neatly inked seeds. Certain pineapples have inked clamshell-like rows, reminiscent of a pineapple's quilted surface. My favorite inked fruit embellishment is to include the tendrils on the grape bunches. Here in Pattern #84, you would first trace the tendrils lightly onto your block in pencil, then go over the lines with a Pigma® .01 pen or a Pilot SC-UF® pen. The trick that makes the difference is to thicken (by going back over) the down stroke (Figure D). From a thin corkscrew line, the down-stroke-thickened tendril becomes artistically weighted, old-fashioned looking, and quite lovely! Review *Volume II*, which goes into informative detail about writing, drawing, and transferring engraved Victorian signature logos onto your quilt blocks—and remember always to heat-set any inkwork and the stencilwork as well.

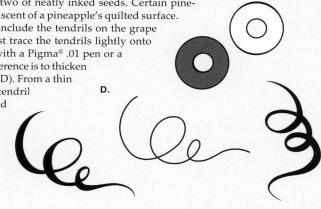

D.

its decreasing saturations of color over a secondary print design. My *Baltimore Beauties®* signature fabric line (produced by P&B Textiles) seeks, and to a great extent achieves, the antique cloth's smooth transitions of hue. But you, yourself, can also capture this exquisite antique textile look, by stenciling.

## PERSONAL STYLE

How happy that the Albums suit such different tastes and talents! Some, like needleartists Kate Fowle (Color Plate #7) and Annette Mahon (Color Plate #4), are skilled reproductionists. Others, like Jeannie Austin (Color Plate #1) and Sue Linker (Color Plate #6) are irrepressibly individualistic. Some can decide exactly which fabrics to use before their appliqué begins. Others find a complex Album block a little overwhelming and need to commit to one fabric choice at a time (for me this is often the greens). Then they let the block "speak to" them, telling them how its style will evolve. Mine is the latter approach, and while my Cornucopia square in Color Plate #3 is unfinished, it has clearly "let me know" how I should proceed.

Annette Mahon reproduced the original Cornucopia, Pattern #49 in the *Pattern Companion to Volume I,* capturing its colors and fabric use remarkably (Color Plate #4). To find my own personal style for that block (Color Plate #3), I first committed to a large green print fabric, using the cut-away appliqué method. While I was at it, I included a leafy bough, seen in another Album Block, across the cornucopia's tip. Anxious about whether the same green print throughout had been simple but unwise, I next chose colorful tie-dyes for the rounded fruits central to the block. A stem-well circle cut from a large print defined them and saved them from looking like croquet balls. Taking my cue from old Albums, I chose shades of solid fabric for the grapes, which ranged from lightest light to definitely dark. This scale of shades depicts the bunch as three-dimensional. The palest grapes appear farthest from the viewer. To this handful of plain colors, I added a subtle print as the final grape. As in antique Albums, this unexpected inclusion adds texture and interest.

In making Album blocks myself, I'm inclined to reinterpretation rather than to reproduction. Thus, when I began the block, I wasn't sure how my fabric choice would proceed. At this point, it has begun to have quite a "painterly" look and seems now to call for a dominant use of solid colors—both plain ones and shaded ones (tie-dyed, stenciled, or printed textiles). From here on, completing my partially sewn block should be fairly straightforward, because it has a clear style all its own, one so distinctive that it dictates a lead I can follow. I would describe its cloth-use mode as predominantly shaded plains with an occasional print accent added.

The tie-dyed plains were chosen with a print window, so that their shading portrays contour, as a painter would shade his paint colors to evoke dimension. In the fall of 1994, P&B Textiles, in my *Baltimore Beauties* signature series, brought out three new printed backgrounds ("Scroll," "Texture," and "Maze"), each with shaded overlays. These prints are the first of their kind since the Album era's rainbow prints. Printed fabrics add a look all quiltmakers love: Now once again, we can have both print and contour in the same cloth. Because fruit shapes tend toward simple, easily sewn lines, you yourself may find that fruit blocks give you a new freedom to explore elements of print and color use as well as an arena for embellishment and personalization. Enjoy this freedom to develop your own unique style as you explore the fruit blocks of old Baltimore.

*Other patterns to make, using techniques learned in this lesson:* Epergne of Fruit III, Pattern #84, and Cornucopia III, Pattern #71, or Vase of Full-Blown Roses II: Rose Amphora, Pattern #72. Any of these squares could as easily hold fruit as flowers. Yet more wonderful fruit blocks grace this series, elsewhere: Fruit in baskets, bowls, horns of plenty, epergnes, and wreaths. Skim the Series' Index at the end of this book for fruit pattern listings. Some blocks in the Color Section, too, are splendid examples made from patterns throughout this series.

Original design may also call to you. It's a natural with fruit! One of my fond dreams is to make a Della Robbia Wreath as an enlarged center medallion. It should be simple enough: Cut a 30" background block, stitch a superfine stem (*Volume I,* page 69, or *Dimensional Appliqué,* Lesson 7, pages 51-52) on a 10" radius around the center. Onto freezer paper, trace fruit shapes from patterns in this series. Then, in paper shapes, lay out the wreath's fruit. Enlarge or reduce the fruit as

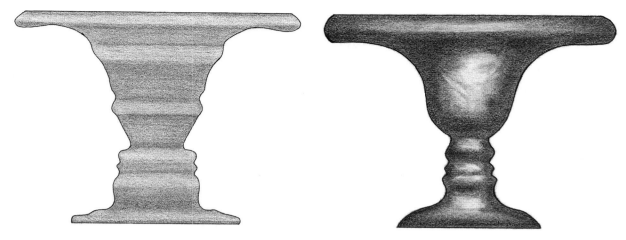

FIGURE 1-11 Portrait Epergnes

necessary and cut them out to arrange on the block. Fill in with foliage, also paper-cut. When the design looks appealing, translate the paper into appliqués prepared in cloth. All that then remains is the pleasure of sitting and stitching! To have a "model" for this, use Pattern #34 from *Dimensional Appliqué.* That pattern is actually for a rose wreath center medallion, inscribed with the Lord's Prayer, from an antique Album.

*Dimensional Appliqué* urged the idea of our reproducing vintage "Baltimore Basket Albums." One could also explore Baltimores that display four blue glass containers around the center, as in Quilt #1. This, too, is a revivalist idea, which warrants expansion. You could even design your own epergnes to personalize the quilt. Ones like the Folk Art Epergne (Template C in Figure 1-3) need no further explanation. But you can get fancier. Years ago, Anita Shackleford shared a vase idea based on optical illusions in art. She had cut her daughter's silhouette, then traced it—facing the fold—for re-cutting. The mirrored image of the space between the silhouettes, appeared at first glance to be a classic raised-glass vase or dish. Anita cut one portrait-vase of each of her daughters, then, filled them with flowers and stitched them into her lovely Shackleford Family Album. Imagine the possibilities! With only honor and no disrespect intended, a Father of Our Country "portrait-epergne" is given in Figure 1-11. At the very least, this concept leads us smoothly—and smiling—into Part Two where pages of paper-cut patterns bloom aplenty!

# PAPERCUTS IN APPLIQUÉ
# PAPERCUTS IN ALBUMS

# INTRODUCTION TO THE LESSONS

At first, the antebellum Baltimores' collective glory left me awestruck. But now, years later, certain Albums shine more brightly in my memory. Perhaps my favorite is the Seidenstricker Papercut Album, first pictured in W. R. Dunton's self-published 1946 classic, *Old Quilts.* Similarly laden with single-layered blocks, Quilt #6, Classic Revival: Alex's Album, pays that prototype homage. Though filled largely with the original's antique patterns, Classic Revival (the needlework of many hands) remains charmingly "beyond Baltimore." A *tour de force* of papercut appliqués, this generous quilt shares the secret of their rich configurations, here.

Boldly, the date "1845" is appliquéd into the Seidenstricker Album's laurel spray border. "1988" and the recipient's initials tie the Classic Revival: Alex's Album border. In each quilt, a wealth of "snowflake" blocks float like festively colored paper doilies. All are set on point and sashed with crisscrossed garlands. Lancaster resident, Sarah Holcomb, too, made a magical Papercut Album in 1847, honoring her friends and relatives. Sarah's Album inspired Quilt #7, Friendship's Offering. Block patterns for this quilt and Classic Revival: Alex's Album are in the Pattern Section while their borders can be found in *Appliqué 12 Borders and Medallions!* Such utterly simple design concepts led to these engaging Albums! Their wondrously diverse blocks spring from just a handful of design formulas. Once grasped, their principles both encourage your creativity and guarantee you graphic success. Short, simple Album block design lessons follow. They aim to inspire an heirloom turn-of-the-century Papercut Album all your own.

## WHAT ARE PAPERCUT ALBUM BLOCKS?

Papercut appliqué has many names including *scherenschnitte* (scissors-cutting) appliqué, snowflake appliqué, whole-cloth or single-layer appliqué, and repeat-image appliqué. We'll use the term "papercut appliqué" most, because for us today, cutting folded freezer paper is the easiest way to create this appliqué design style. The process is always the same: One folds the paper and cuts a shape drawn on the top layer. When the paper is opened up, the cut surfaces mirror each other across the folds, creating eye-catchingly fresh patterns. Traditionally, the basic differences in papercut designs are in the paper used and in the number of folds.

Since our finished shape will be out of cloth, not paper, the critical difference for us is in the number of folds. The folds create layers of paper, which are cut simultaneously. Each layer forms one repeat of the design drawn on the top layer.

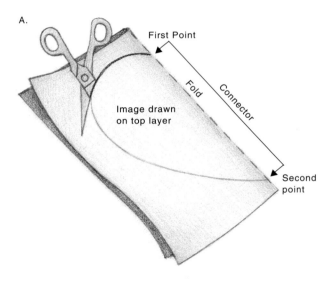

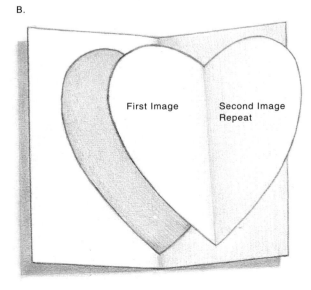

FIGURE 2-1A–B Cutting a Two-Repeat Pattern

C.

FIGURE 2-1C A Two-Repeat Pattern from *Spoken Without a Word.*

each other. Quilt blocks tend to be single-fold (two-image) patterns (Figure 2-1B, C) or eight-fold (eight-image) patterns (Figure 2-2C, D).

While repeat-image patterns surely do sparkle distinctively from Baltimore's Albums, the question of what first was folded to cut the designs—paper or cloth—is unresolved. Wouldn't it be fun to find one of these papercut blocks "in progress" from old Baltimore so that we would know more? The crossed sprays of one unfinished antique appliqué block (Plate 20 of Ruth Finley's *Old Patchwork Quilts and the Women Who Made Them*, 1929) descend in size, as though they were cut directly out of folded cloth, and then basted to the background. Appliqués cut from eight-fold cloth seem to have been popular, both here and in Britain, in the first third of the 19th century. Today, too, this appliqué tradition still flourishes in Hawaii. But part of old Baltimore's distinctive brilliance is in the detailed wonderment—the astonishing intricacy—of her fancier blocks. Her most elaborate repeat-image designs must surely have been cut first in paper.

The design must extend from fold line to fold line at a minimum of two points (Figure 2-1A). The width between the two drawn points is the "connector," which keeps all the layers, when cut, connected to

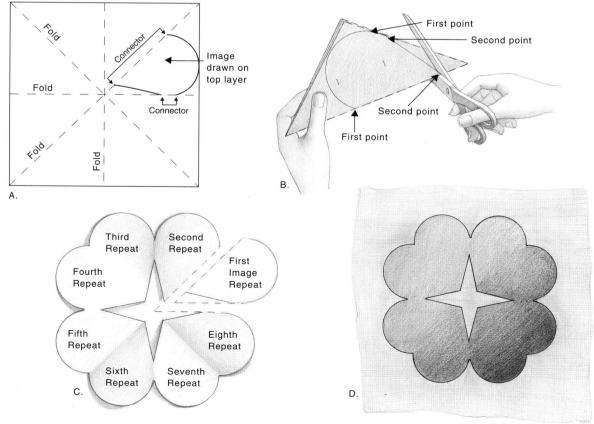

FIGURE 2-2A–D Cutting an Eight-Repeat Pattern out of paper.

## HOW IS A PAPERCUT PATTERN TRANSLATED INTO CLOTH?

A papercut block design sewn by the Freezer Paper on Top appliqué method is the perfect technological marriage! Here's how it is done: The design (either one from this book or your original) is cut from folded freezer paper, then ironed heavily so that the plastic coating melds the paper to the right side of the appliqué cloth. You pin this paper-marked appliqué layer to the background cloth, then cut the seam incrementally, just ahead of the sewing. This method is well illustrated in *Baltimore Beauties and Beyond, Volume I*, on pages 50-51. Album teacher Gail Kessler suggests using clear, self-adhering Con-Tact® Paper for papercut pattern templates, rather than freezer paper. A clever alternative, Con-Tact Paper's transparency allows you to position the pattern in just that area of a large print that most enhances its shape. The actual stitching of papercut appliqués is uniquely straightforward since no layering of appliqué cloth is required. One can even do these papercut appliqués as fused cut-outs by blanket-stitching their raw edges. This couldn't be easier! Learn all about that utterly simple method on *Volume I's* pages 101-102. Following *Volume I's* introductory lessons and stitching instructions—as you progress from this book's simpler patterns to its more challenging ones—is a recipe for honing your appliqué skills to perfection!

"Freezer paper on top" was probably not precisely the 19th-century way. Not only was there no freezer paper (though in China, paper is still adhered to needlework cloth with flour paste) but the cut-away appliqué method requires a whole piece of appliqué cloth at least a bit larger than the design. Perhaps a less-consuming age might have found the method a bit wasteful? Sometimes, in Baltimore's simpler papercuts, the appliqué fabric has been thriftily pieced, as though to extend same-cloth scraps sufficiently to make the full pattern. Lucky for us, appliqué by freezer paper on top makes breathtaking heirloom appliqué feasible—and even easy.

## MATERIALS NEEDED FOR THE LESSONS

- Freezer paper both for paperfolding and pattern transfer: Precut the paper into 12½" squares. This is the standard pattern design area used throughout the *Baltimore Beauties* series.

- Pencil and fine felt-tipped pen for sketching the image on the top layer of folded paper.

- Rulers: One gridded straight-edge; one flexible edge for drawing curves.

- Circle templates and photocopied images: Gather any templates and pictures that will help you create your own original pattern images.

- Repositionable glue stick or repositionable tape (available at art or office supply stores): Complex papercutting can involve pasting up a design's component elements when simply drawing them does not suffice.

- Light box: When the subject exceeds your draftsmanship, simply trace representational motifs (photocopied from another source) onto your paper block mockup. Upsize or downsize pictures (to fit the surface between the folds) by using a photocopier. Even photographs can lead to suitable papercuts when just the silhouette (the outline) of the subject is used.

- Stapler and staple-remover: Staple the paperfold's layers together so they won't shift when you cut through all.

- 5" Paper scissors: Sturdy Gingher® Tailor-Point Scissors are ideal because they cut cleanly and to-the-point through eight layers of paper.

# LESSON 3

## FUNDAMENTALS OF PAPERCUT DESIGN— MAKING A TWO-REPEAT PAPERCUT BLOCK

### PATTERN:
Designing an Original Two-Repeat Block

Papercutting is an old, old art form beloved in both European and Asian cultures. The purvey of both the folk and the professional, this craft, like quiltmaking itself, is filled with tradition. Sometimes the paper is cut flat, with a knife. Sometimes the paper is cut folded with scissors. Baltimore's heavy German influx in the mid-19th century is no doubt reflected in her *scherenschnitte*-like Album blocks. The simplest paperfold patterns are two-repeat designs, like the Valentine heart so prevalent in Germanic folk art. Diverse hearts, symbolic of Devotion or Love, are common in the classic Albums. Let's familiarize ourselves with papercut patterns by designing a heart motif block. Keep in mind that though simple, hearts can be problematical: The heart's top-heaviness needs careful placement in an Album's overall set. For reasons both of ease and of challenge then, a heart seems the perfect place to start!

### EXERCISE 1: CUTTING A HEART MOTIF ALBUM BLOCK

#### Making the Pattern's Basic Heart Template

1. Fold a 12½" freezer paper square in half vertically, plastic-coated side in. This fold marks the vertical center of the design as in Figure 2-1A and B on page 38.

2. Sketch half a heart on the top layer. The outside of the heart faces the raw edges of the paper; the inside faces the fold. This basic heart template should pretty much fill the block, touching the paper's edges or coming to within ¼" of them.

3. Staple twice inside the heart you've just drawn, so that the layers don't shift. Then cut it out. When you're pleased with the basic heart template, cut a duplicate (Figure 2-3A). Use this duplicate to cut the heart template further in Step #4. (Keep the original for insurance—or to make yet more same-heart Album block designs.)

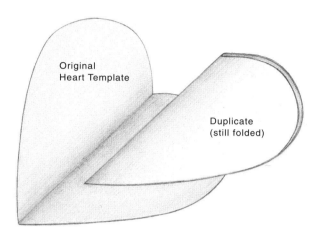

Original Heart Template

Duplicate (still folded)

FIGURE 2-3A

### Ornamenting the Heart

4. Victorian Album blocks have an elegant tenor. To be "Victorian" in aspect, our so-basic heart hungers for style-giving ornament. Favorite folk art decorations outline the heart with geometrical repeats or botanical elements (Figure 2-3B).

   Since no scalloped heart has graced our *Baltimore Beauties* series, let's design one here. Create three interior guidelines for the ornamentation by echo-cutting smaller hearts within the duplicate heart template. Trace these outlines onto a fresh freezer paper square. Use two of the outlines as a baseline on which to draw your scallops (Figure 2-3C).

5. Use a circle template to make the scallops. Draw them onto the right-hand side of the freezer paper pattern, then repeat them by tracing their outline (over a light box) onto the left side of the pattern (Figure 2-3D).

   Alternatively you can stack-cut a set of circles, cut them in half for scallops, then arrange these cutouts artfully along a heart baseline. Tape (repositionable tape) the scallops in place on the right half of the heart pattern. Then retrace the idealized outline onto another square of freezer paper. Use a light box for the initial tracing, then again to repeat the drawing thus obtained, on the left half of the pattern. When you're pleased with your fancified heart, leave a clean tracing of it drawn on a folded-paper square, but not cut out (Figure 2-3D, also). This becomes your master pattern.

FIGURE 2-3B

"Heart Wreath with Buds" pattern from *Design a Baltimore Album Quilt*

"Friendship is a Sheltering Tree" pattern from *Appliqué 12 Easy Ways!*

"Wreathed Heart" pattern from *Spoken Without a Word*

FIGURE 2-3C

This space available for corner motif.

FIGURE 2-3D

FIGURE 2-3E

## EXERCISE 2: ADDING A BALANCING MOTIF AT THE BOTTOM OF THE HEART BLOCK

Consider your design's position on an Album block. Here's where the challenge comes in! While a heart is an endearing motif, it fills the top of the quilt square pleasingly, but leaves the bottom half disproportionately empty. This poses symmetry problems in your quilt's set. An even number of Heart-only blocks gives your quilt a visually strong rhythmical element. *(Design a Baltimore Album Quilt!* explains this concept well. A beautiful quilt on its back cover repeats eight heart-wreaths in a recognizable pattern. You can see a full-size version of this quilt, #3, here in the color section.) To make a heart design fit in easily with all sorts of Album blocks, its empty bottom corners need motifs that balance the top. Here's how we'll go about adding such elements:

1.  Fold up a master pattern bottom corner, to delineate the space available for a corner motif (Figure 2-3D, also).

2.  Onto the master pattern, trace a motif tailored to size. Figure 2-3E, for instance, shows our scalloped heart now nestled between gloved hands. (Recalling the Album era's "heart and hand" theme seems perennially pleasant!)

3.  If you want to keep the master pattern intact, make a copy to cut for transferring the design to your appliqué cloth: Trace the right-hand half of the pattern onto the right-hand side of a freezer paper square, folded in half, plastic-coated side inside. Draw two temporary "pattern bridges" connecting the inner heart to the outer heart, and the outer heart to the glove. These pattern bridges are simply ¼" wide tabs that connect the pattern's separate pieces (like a paper doily) long enough to iron them in position on the appliqué cloth. At that point, the temporary bridges can be snipped off. This pattern transfer concept is well explained in *Volume I*, pages 39-40, and 45.

# LESSON 4

## ELABORATIONS:
## EIGHT-REPEAT
## ALBUM BLOCK DESIGN

Both antique Papercut Albums and their contemporary sisters sparkle with eight-repeat patterns. We know this style from childhood. As quiltmakers now, we are even more keenly aware of this mirrored design's potential. Papercutting's wonder-working, we find, far exceeds the crystalline abstraction of snowflakes. Papercuts are eminently successful at creating ornamental patterns from realistic images as well. These realistic or representational patterns can be made by a variety of simple design formulas. Rather than have you develop your own design immediately, as in Lesson 3, we'll look together at blocks from the Pattern Sections, which illustrate each formula. Then, after studying these models, you'll have both the inspiration and the tools to try each formula on a design of your own. But first, turn to the Color Section and savor there the unique aesthetic of Papercut Albums. Though old, the style remains extraordinarily fresh to us. As an Album style, its lines are clean and graphic. And as a quiltmaker's "collection on a theme," Snowflake Albums convey significant meaning with unparalleled ease.

## EIGHT-REPEAT PATTERNS

Eight-repeat patterns outnumber all other forms of papercut appliqué designs and seemingly have, throughout the American quilt's evolution. The eight-repeat cutout applied to quiltmaking must have migrated from Europe to North America and on to Hawaii. Even the mainland's perennial crossed sprays and symmetrical wreath patterns are eight-repeat designs. Old favorites like Crossed Laurel Sprays, the Rose of Sharon, and President's Wreath are all-pervasive in appliqué quilts. But in the classic Baltimores, crossed sprays and even wreaths often have a unique look, now so familiar to us all.

Western culture's taste for the traditional symmetry of mirrored-image designs has been enduring. And their creation is seductively easy. What one draws, even sketchily, can be cut smoothly through eight layers, then magically unfolded into a more beautiful whole. All school children know well the delight of cutting snowflakes, whereby a casual cutting pattern transforms plain paper into the mysteries of the universe, captured on a thread or taped to a window.

A. "Fleur-de-Lis with Maple Leaves" pattern from *Design a Baltimore Album Quilt!*

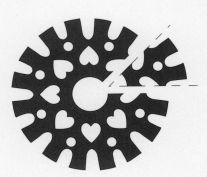

B. "Wheel of Hearts" pattern from
*Spoken Without a Word*

C. "Tender Tulips" pattern from
*Design a Baltimore Album Quilt*

# PAPER-FOLDING FOR EIGHT-REPEAT PATTERN DESIGN AND TRANSFER

1.  Fold the freezer paper square in half, folding from left to right with the shiny side inside. Align all edges.

2.  Fold the square into fourths, folding from the bottom to the top.

3.  Fold the square into eighths. Begin by folding the front flap foreward: Fold the upper left to lower right.

4.  Next fold the back flap to the back, upper left to the lower right. As this triangle faces you now, mark a C for center, where the folds meet. Mark an E for edge at the top of the triangle. Draw the pattern's image on the top layer of the triangle from fold to fold.

5.  Staple, then cut through all layers. Remove the staples and unfold the design. The wedge on which you drew the heart is surrounded by a dashed line.

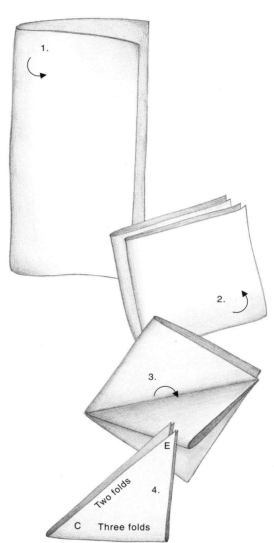

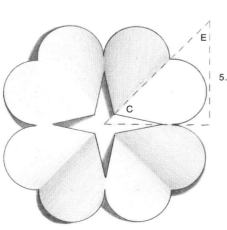

*Instructions and several options for transferring such a pattern to your cloth are given in* Volume I, *pages 21-25.*

# FROM ANCIENT GREECE TO MODERN ALBUMS!

Geometric designs and mirrored botanical appliqués dance gaily in vintage Papercut Albums. Patterns recur often, probably both through sharing and through individuals' original papercuts of favorite motifs. Some motifs seem repeated because of their significance, like the popular Fleur-de-Lis and perhaps the neoclassic palmetto motif. The palmetto or "shell" emblem is ancient. It tops the Parthenon's tiles, and has decorated Western artifacts for centuries. As in the antique Baltimore Seidenstricker Album, a palmetto knots the contemporary Classic Revival: Alex's Album border (detail shown below; also see Quilt #6 in the Color Section that begins on page 57). Here, it ties this ancient motif to the quilts of this century and yet another to come. Both the Seidenstricker Album and this new one sport impressively intricate "palmetto frame" blocks as well. In the Classic Revival: Alex's Album, five of them frame family portraits.

The venerable palmetto or shell motif, familiar to us on both American and European furnishings, forms the uppermost decorative edging on the marble tiles of the Parthenon. Engraving by L. Vulliamy, from Owen Jones, *The Grammar of Ornament*, England, 1856.

## REPRESENTATIONAL PAPERCUTS

In the papercuts of modern Albums, you'll see intriguing representational blocks, which include figurative elements. Quilts #11, 12, 13, and 15 were designed and made by Kathie Campbell and Ann Sheridan, each for one of their daughters. Into heirloom Albums, they've stitched remembrances of school trips, special pets, the front yard tree gazed out upon through all those growing-up years, memories of afternoon teas, gymnastics, and a fondness for Mickey Mouse. They've also updated quiltmaking's papercuts to yet another century. In these Albums, original patterns co-mingle with oft-repeated traditional designs. By such artifice, then, we thread our lives into a powerful continuum and wrap our loved ones with comfort.

By now we're familiar with the use of symbolism in the antique Albums and have, ourselves, developed a fondness for this means of expression. We luxuriate in the freedom to convey some things realistically and other things through emblems with a significance known, perhaps, only to ourselves. Surely many representational antique Album blocks have meanings, now long forgotten. Sarah Holcomb's fresh botanical blocks, though, still sing clear praises of plenty. With a clever artistry, she cut stylized plants into cohesive block designs, which suit an Album's collection perfectly. Proving that imitation is indeed the "sincerest form of flattery," echoes of Sarah's botanical blocks fill contemporary Quilt #7, Friendship's Offering. To the already magnificent 19th-century Papercut Album format, modern quiltmakers have added both a flurry of their own fine penwork and the zest of original figurative designs. Look for contemporary snowflake blocks with dogs, cats, angels, kangaroos, swans, turtles, houses, violins, hands, teddy bears, the Eiffel Tower—and more—in the Color Section's quilts. Then, in the Pattern Section, find a treasure-hunt's worth of ready-to-use antique and contemporary papercut patterns.

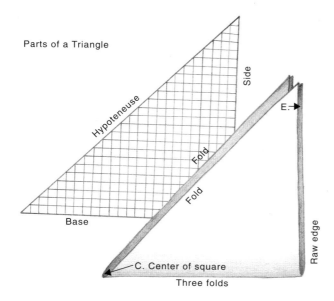

Parts of a Triangle

FIGURE 2-4  Triangle for Drawing an Eight-Repeat Pattern: Orient the folded freezer-paper square in this position while drawing the pattern repeat on its top layer. The folded triangle shown here represents the wedge removed from the pattern in Figure 2-2C and throughout this lesson. We'll refer to the parts of the triangle as labeled here. "C" marks the block's center, while "E" points to the raw edges. In the Pattern Section, too, centers and edges are identified for ease in pasting the photocopy of each pattern quadrant onto an eight-fold freezer-paper square.

## PRINCIPLES OF EIGHT-REPEAT ALBUM BLOCK DESIGN

You can design an entire Album of original papercut blocks. Modern technology—photocopiers for changing a pattern's size, light boxes for tracing, and our wealth of printed graphic images—combines so easily with this lesson's simple papercut design formulas—so much so that contemporary Papercut Albums can even aspire to outshine their antique sisters. Here are the basic principles of papercut appliqué design:

- The freezer paper square you fold is always the size of the finished block's design area. In the *Baltimore Beauties* series, this is always a 12½" square. (Sometimes that design image is appliquéd onto a bigger block, perhaps a 14" one, or even a 16" square. In this book, however, the papercut patterns tend to have a bit more white space around them, so that the finished block size can be cut down to 11½". This was done so that a quilt with lots of papercut blocks does not become overly large.)

- To cut patterns of a uniform size (11½" square, for example), make sure the drawn design always comes to the same distance away from the freezer paper square's edges. When the square is folded, the paper's raw edges form the triangle's side (Figure 2-4).

- To have the eight-image repeats hold together, make sure that the design remains attached to both folds. (See Figure 2-2B on page 39.)

- *Options:* The papercut design can be focused on the hypoteneuse (the side opposite the right angle—the longest fold) of the triangle or on its base, or in the space between this set of folds. While papercut block designs are always initially cut symmetrically, elements within them can be re-cut, asymmetrically. For Album Quilts, you want an open, signable block center. You're also seeking a pleasing outer edge profile so that the appliqué reads decoratively against the background cloth.

Let's treat these various design principles as though they were formulas for achieving diverse effects. When the resulting patterns are combined they will create such an utterly bewitching quilt!

## PAPERCUTTING FORMULAS FOR EIGHT-REPEAT ALBUM BLOCK DESIGN

### FORMULA #1:
### PLACE THE MAIN DESIGN FOCUS ON THE HYPOTENEUSE.

In Devon Violets for Nana (Virginia Griswold Ferris) (Figure 2-5, Pattern #51), the papercut's main design focus (the flower and buds) is drawn on the hypotenuse. The secondary design (the leaf) is drawn on the triangle's base, while the connective element (a wreath of hearts) joins the hypoteneuse to the base. The space between the triangle's point and the connective element is always cut away so that open space is left for the Album inscription. Watch for the pleasingly different signature centers that result from diverse cutting patterns.

For an interesting twist on the "main design on the hypoteneuse" formula, see Figure 2-6 George Washington's Redbud (Pattern #38). By contrast to the Devon Violets design, this papercut's main focus is the graceful Redbud leaf, not the buds themselves. The leaf, therefore, is drawn on the hypoteneuse. The secondary design (the buds) is drawn on the triangle's base, while the connective element (hearts, also) joins the hypoteneuse folds to the base folds.

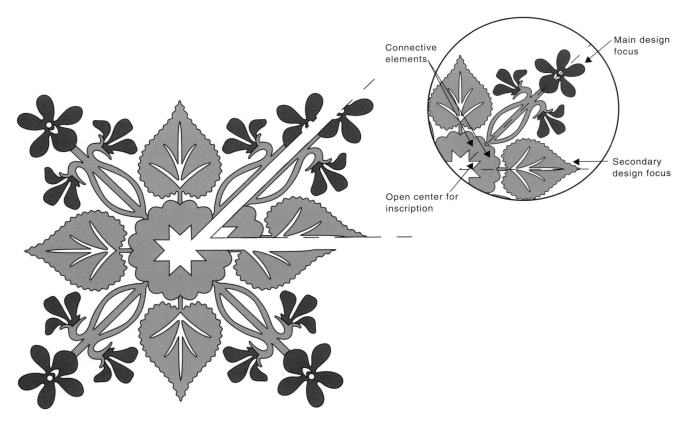

FIGURE 2-5  **Papercut Formula 1: Place the Main Design Focus on the Hypoteneuse.**
Illustrated by Devon Violets for Nana, Pattern #51, Block F-3 from the quilt, Classic Revival: Alex's Album.

## FORMULA #1 (continued)

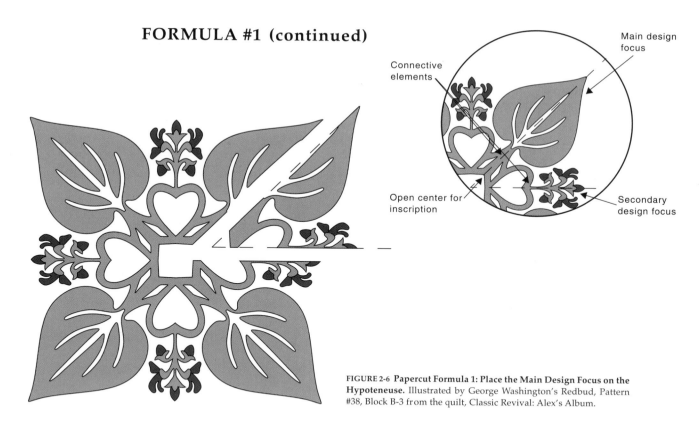

FIGURE 2-6 **Papercut Formula 1: Place the Main Design Focus on the Hypoteneuse.** Illustrated by George Washington's Redbud, Pattern #38, Block B-3 from the quilt, Classic Revival: Alex's Album.

## FORMULA #2: ADD A SECOND COLOR.

Devon Violets for Nana and George Washington's Redbud are both designs that work beautifully as silhouettes (shapes cut from a single layer of cloth). In both patterns, however, the block has been drawn so that it can be sewn in a dominant color with a secondary accent color for the violets, buds, and/or the heart wreath. A place for secondary colors is easily made by drawing a line that isolates one appliqué element from another. George Washington's red-buds (Figure 2-7) have been delineated from the calyx, while Nana's violet blossom is drawn separate from its stem. In both blooms, the second color is added after the main color has been sewn down by cut-away appliqué. The redbud is slipped under a calyx, left open to receive it, while the violet covers the stem's raw-edged tip. For a lesson devoted to the technique of adding a second color to cut-away appliqué, see *Volume I's* Lesson 5.

If you prefer both the visual and technical complexity of multiple fabrics and colors, you can still do papercuts to design the block's overall layout. (Papercuts make such captivating designs!) From the master pattern thus cut, you can then work at separating the overall pattern into elements for separate fabric appliqué or for reverse appliqué.

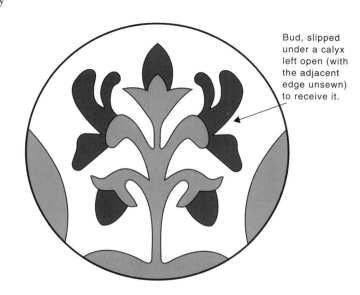

FIGURE 2-7 **Papercut Formula 2: Add a Second Color.** Illustrated by George Washington's Redbud (Detail of Pattern #38).

# FORMULA #3:
## PLACE THE MAIN DESIGN FOCUS BETWEEN THE TRIANGLE'S BASE AND ITS HYPOTENEUSE.

In Alex's Cats (Figure 2-8, Pattern #36), the papercut's main design focus (the cat) is drawn centered within the triangle. Its body rests on the side while its ears touch the hypoteneuse. The secondary design (the initial "A" for Alex, augmented by a heart motif) is centered on the triangle's base. It personalizes the design and serves as a secondary design. The hearts connect the hypoteneuse folds to the base folds. In a happy configuration, their tips form a starry signature frame at the block's center. The cat is a "found image" taken from an antique silhouette. A photocopy of the cat was sized to fit so that it could be traced onto the pattern's triangle. The cat is also an asymmetrical motif. For both asymmetrical motifs and found elements, central placement on the triangle is ideal.

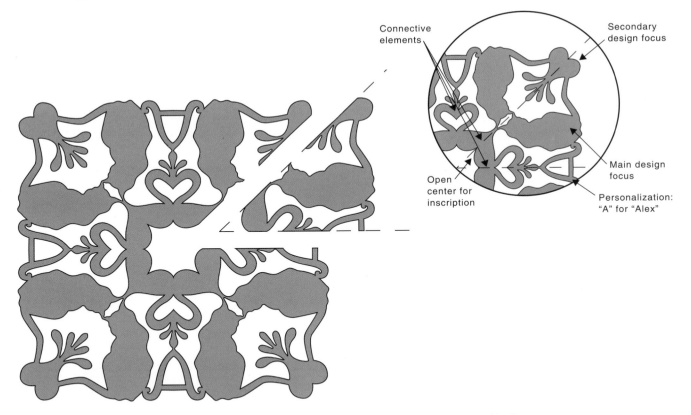

FIGURE 2-8  **Papercut Formula 3: Place the Main Design Focus Between the Triangle's Base and its Hypoteneuse.**
Illustrated by Alex's Cats, Pattern #36, Block B-1 from the quilt, Classic Revival: Alex's Album.

# FORMULA #4:
## PLACE THE MAIN DESIGN FOCUS ON BOTH THE SIDE AND THE HYPOTENEUSE.

In Landon Bears Football Team (Figure 2-9, Pattern #54), the papercut's main design focus (the bear) is drawn twice, once centered on the hypotenuse and again on the base. This design, symmetrically placed on both folds, creates a 16-repeat pattern, but without having to cut through the bulk of 16 layers. To position the bears at the same level on both folds, a semi-circle was drawn with the point of the compass placed at the center of the folded square.

The secondary design (the nickname "Al," disguised as protective football gear) falls on the line that bisects the triangle's hypoteneuse and base. The asymmetrical initial "L" should be cut only partially, initially. Just the base of the letter was cut symmetrically on each fold for each bear. The pattern was then opened to four repeats and the vertical left side of the letters were cut through four layers only. The result is 16 Bears bearing the team letter "L."

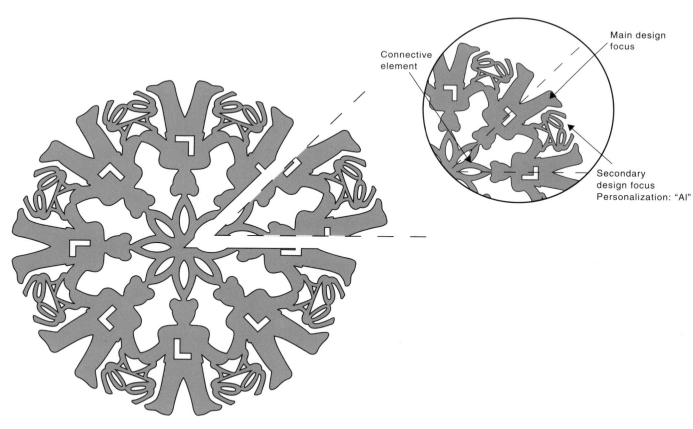

**FIGURE 2-9  Papercut Formula 4: Place the Main Design Focus on Both the Side and the Hypotenuese.**
Illustrated by Landon Bears Football Team, Pattern #54, Block G-2 from the quilt, Classic Revival: Alex's Album.

# FORMULA #5: INCORPORATE A "FOUND" FIGURATIVE MOTIF INTO YOUR PAPERCUT.

Look for pictures from simple outlines to photographs, which will make an evocative silhouette. It is the motif's outline that, when fabric-filled, determines how intriguing a representational Album block will be. In the case of the Cherubs (Pattern #22), this shape (Figure 2-10A) is an old, possibly Victorian one. It first caught my eye for use on a Valentine card for my husband. The same evocative shape was called into service again when I wanted to include a symbolic angel in Sue Hannan's birthday quilt, Friendship's Offering (Quilt #7). For that purpose, I reduced the shape to fit within a triangle, one eighth of the desired quilt-block size. Following childhood's paperdoll principle, I knew that the angel had to touch both folded edges (both the triangle's base and its hypoteneuse)

so that the design, once cut, would remain all in one piece. (When I was a little girl I remember repeating silently to myself: "The paperdolls have to hold hands from fold to fold, or they will fall apart!")

This papercut's main design focus (the cherub) was drawn centered within the triangle. Its body rests on the hypoteneuse while its arrow touches the base. Connective elements (hearts) join the hypoteneuse to the base. Yet another heart motif at the cherub's feet serves to extend this design the full length of the hypoteneuse, ensuring that it fills the finished square fully.

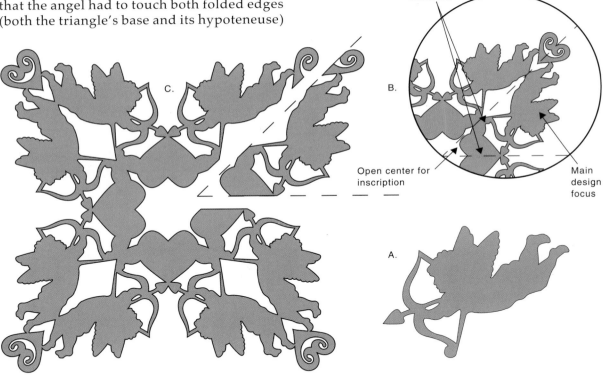

FIGURE 2-10A-C Papercut Formula 5: Incorporate a "Found" Figurative Motif into Your Papercut.
Illustrated by Cherubs, Pattern #22, Block E-2 from the quilt, Classic Revival: Alex's Album.

# FORMULA #6: ADD ASYMMETRY TO YOUR PAPERCUT.

Balanced asymmetry seems to have been beloved by the Album makers. To get this effect in your papercuts, change at least one element of a symmetrically cut design into an asymmetrical element. Thus, in Pattern #13, Cabin Fever Calicoes, the house has first to be cut symmetri-

cally through all eight layers (Figure 2-11A). After this initial symmetrical cut, the pattern was opened into quarters. Then the asymmetrical interior of the house outline (windows, door, and roof line) was redrawn and a second four-layer cutting was made. (Figure 2-11B). The papercut's

# FORMULA #6 (continued)

main design focus (the house) is drawn centered on the hypoteneuse. Curling chimney-smoke touches the heart wreath that connects the triangle's hypoteneuse to its base.

In the asymmetrical pattern Hearts and Hands (Figure 2-12C, Pattern #14), the papercut's main design focus (the hand) is drawn centered on the hypoteneuse. A ruffled wristcuff touches a secondary motif (a needle drawn on the triangle's base) and connects all the motifs in the layout. The hand was first cut as a symmetrical hand with five fingers (Figure 2-12A). To add the asymmetrical thumb, the pattern was opened flat. The left-most finger was then redrawn into a thumb (Figure 2-12B), and the pattern recut as a four-image repeat. The heart, hand, needle, and twined thread motif symbolize, of course, a needleworker.

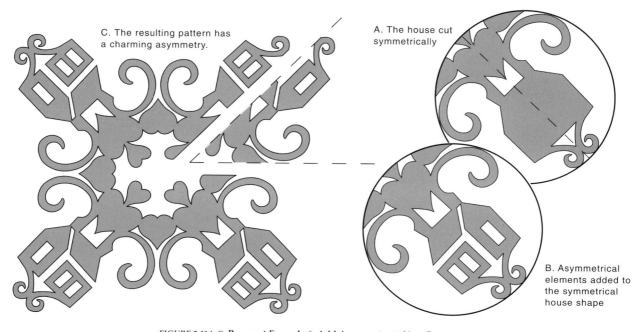

C. The resulting pattern has a charming asymmetry.

A. The house cut symmetrically

B. Asymmetrical elements added to the symmetrical house shape

**FIGURE 2-11A-C  Papercut Formula 6: Add Asymmetry to Your Papercut.**
Illustrated by Friendship's Offering, Pattern #13, Block C-2 from the quilt, Friendship's Offering.

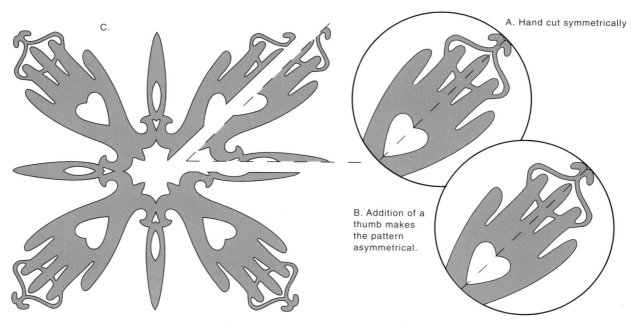

C.

A. Hand cut symmetrically

B. Addition of a thumb makes the pattern asymmetrical.

**FIGURE 2-12A-C  Papercut Formula 6: Add Asymmetry to Your Papercut.**
Illustrated by Hearts and Hands, Pattern #14, Block C-5 from the quilt, Friendship's Offering.

## FINISHING TOUCHES: INKED ALBUM BLOCK EMBELLISHMENTS

Personal blessings—those of cherished people drawn close 'round her—seem well counted in the antique Sarah Holcomb Album. For in addition to being composed largely of papercuts, both the Seidenstricker Album and the Holcomb Album seem to be Remembrance Albums carrying, as they do, friends' and family's names. Time has turned those careful inscriptions from black to a dark chocolate brown. Now, with an ease not possible 150 years ago, you can pen both sentiment and beauty onto your own Album. Anyone-can-do-it directions (plus a Copperplate calligraphy alphabet) for writing on your blocks in Album-style script are given in *Volume II's* Chapter 2. The same antique motifs, which appear to have been "engraved" (die-printed) on antebellum Albums, are in *Volume II,* ready to be transferred to cloth with the help of a photocopier. As we've seen, the familiar open Album block centers are charmingly varied. They await your pen's finishing touch!

## THE FORMULA FOR A PAPERCUT ALBUM QUILT.

You can happily mix papercut-style appliqué blocks with layered Album blocks. They show each other off to advantage. But when the quilt is composed mostly or entirely of snowflake cut blocks, it has a cohesiveness not easily come by in other Baltimore-style Albums. This cohesiveness is even more emphatic when the appliqués are done in one or two colors. The drama so critical to a great quilt is added by the set, border, quilting, and binding. A simple three-part design formula for Papercut Albums follows:

1. **Color:**
   In 19th-century Papercut Albums, the color schemes tended to feature two high-contrast colors (such as red and green) on a neutral background. A tiny splash of a fourth accent color was used to spectacular effect. The yellow in Friendship's Offering (Quilt #7), for example, seems a touch of genius.

2. **Block Design:**
   Keep the blocks predominantly one-layer papercut appliqués. A second fabric is occasionally incorporated into the block design, as an accent. The appliqués' shapes (square, round, diamond-shaped, etc.) on the block can vary. The pattern's shape on the block determines the proportion of positive (appliqué) space to negative (background) space. Exercises in *Design a Baltimore Album Quilt!* refine your expertise in manipulating the positive/negative space into an important quilt set element.

3. **Set:**
   A strong set and border are needed for your Album's forceful visual presentation. Since the snowflake-like appearance of the blocks tends to be soothingly concordant, the pattern in which the blocks are set together becomes particularly important. All the myriad elements that may be critical to a memorable set are well reviewed in the author's *Design a Baltimore Album Quilt!*

## ADD SIGNIFICANCE: PERSONALIZE YOUR DESIGN!

Try personalizing your papercut by incorporating significant letters: an initial, a name, or a monogram. A monogram (two or more letters of a name in a single decorative motif) or a complete name of few letters could, in fact, form the main design focus. In Alex's Cats (Figure 2-8) and in Landon Bears (Figure 2-9), the initial "A" and a nickname, "Al," serve simply as the kind of tucked-in secret symbol, which seems to have gratified quiltmakers since the craft began.

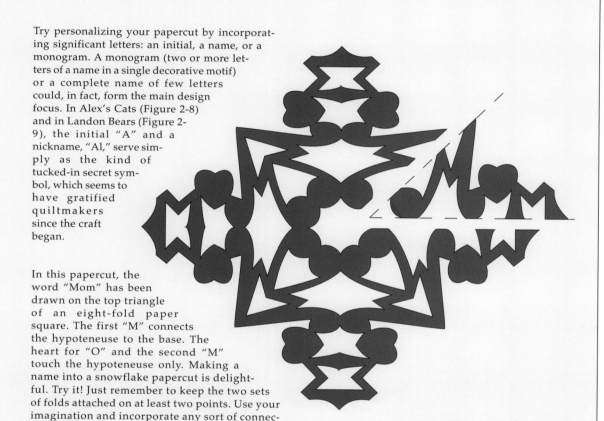

In this papercut, the word "Mom" has been drawn on the top triangle of an eight-fold paper square. The first "M" connects the hypoteneuse to the base. The heart for "O" and the second "M" touch the hypoteneuse only. Making a name into a snowflake papercut is delightful. Try it! Just remember to keep the two sets of folds attached on at least two points. Use your imagination and incorporate any sort of connective elements that can make this happen.

**Snowflake Cut of "Mom"**

# SYMBOLISM: ADDED MEANING
# IN ALBUM BLOCK IMAGES

As in so many Album blocks, all the elements of the design *E Pluribus Unum: Eagles and Oaks* (Pattern #46) have beneficent connotations. The eagle, as the United States' national emblem, conveys allegiance in this pattern. As an ancient symbol it also carries older, broader meanings: Courage, Generosity, Highest Inspiration, and Resurrection. An oak branch means Victory and oak leaves connote Courage, while acorns convey Longevity and Immortality. The use of symbols (visible signs of invisible things) is integral to quiltmaking. Perhaps a look through a dictionary of symbols *(Spoken Without a Word,* for example) will inspire original design papercuts from your hand!

In this asymmetrical pattern, the papercut's main design focus (the eagle) is drawn centered on the hypoteneuse. (When that first cutting was opened flat, there were two heads and three feet. One head was cut off in the shape of a feathered back, and the right-hand foot was cut into tail feathers.) The eagle's wings touch the triangle's base. The secondary design of oak leaves and acorns joins the triangle's hypoteneuse and the base. As a connector, it serves the purpose both of defining the block's signature center and of adding yet more sentiment and symbolism to this patriotic design.

# COLOR SECTION
# THE PLEASURES OF PLENTY

With an impassioned lyricism, Baltimore Albums extolled the Fruits of the Earth. Echoes of those poetic voices can once more be heard in contemporary fruit-filled Album blocks. Such offerings, both new and old are pictured here.

1. SCALLOPED EPERGNE (Pattern #44 in *Baltimore Album Quilts)*. Jeannie Austin. (Photo: Sharon Risedorph)

2. EPERGNE OF FRUIT IV (Pattern #85). Wendy Grande. A wealth of little-known needlework techniques stars in Wendy's Fruit Bowl. Their secrets are shared in Part One. (Photo: Jack Mathieson)

1

2

3

4

5

3. CORNUCOPIA (version of Pattern #49 in *Baltimore Album Quilts)*. Block in-progress by the author. Here, the foliage was stitched by cut-away appliqué. The fruit, done by the Freezer Paper Inside method, is beginning to define the block's style. It seems to be "telling" the maker to use predominantly tie-dyed cloth with the occasional print, and to thereby enhance the "painterly look," which it has already begun to assume. The freezer paper pattern ironed to the cornucopia will be cut into separate templates for Freezer Paper Inside appliqué. (Photo: S. Risedorph)

4. CORNUCOPIA II (Pattern #49 in *Baltimore Album Quilts)*. Annette Mahon. (Photo: S. Risedorph)

5. CORNUCOPIA. Detail from a Classic Baltimore Album Quilt (pictured in full in this book's sequel), which has descended in the Fulford family. (Photo: Courtesy of Nancy Fulford)

6

6. SCALLOPED EPERGNE (Pattern #44 in *Baltimore Album Quilts*). Sue Linker. (Photo: S. Risedorph)

7. EPERGNE OF FRUIT III (Pattern #84). Kate Fowle. (Photo: S. Risedorph)

8. EPERGNE (No pattern) from a Classic Baltimore Album Quilt (pictured in full in this book's sequel) descended in the Fulford family. (Photo: Courtesy of N. Fulford)

7

8

9

10

9. BASKET OF FRUIT
(No pattern) from a
Classic Baltimore Album
Quilt (pictured in full in
this book's sequel)
descended in the Fugate
family. (Photo: Courtesy
of Elaine Fugate)

10. BASKET OF FRUIT
(No pattern) from a
Classic Baltimore Album
Quilt in the Fugate family.
(Photo: Courtesy of
E. Fugate)

11. URN OF FRUIT
(No pattern) from a
Classic Baltimore Album
Quilt in the Fugate family.
(Photo: Courtesy of
E. Fugate)

11

# A Plethora of Album Blocks

Our journey to Baltimore and Beyond has
included lessons both in how to design
and how to execute appliqué. This
portion of the Color Section opens with
the inspiration of two blocks patterned
elsewhere, then goes on to picture a
wealth of blocks whose patterns are given
in this book. Wonderful group quilts
made from patterns in this series illustrate yet more blocks and suggest how
such squares may be set together.

12

12. *SCHERENSCHNITTE* HEART
("From a pattern by Mary
W. Heart in *Country
Handcrafts*"). Dixie
Haywood. This modern
appliquéd Album block
beautifully illustrates the
promise of papercuts and
appliqué! (Photo:
S. Risedorph)

13. PROMISES (Pattern in
*Appliqué 12 Easy Ways!*).
Original border papercut
design by the author. This
is a "picture" block with
traditional figures, beautifully hand-appliquéd by
Sue Hale. (Photo:
S. Risedorph)

13

14

15

16

14. RED BIRD ON A PASSION FLOWER BRANCH
(Pattern #82). Ginni Berg. (Photo S. Risedorph)

15. BASKET OF FULL-BLOWN ROSES (Pattern #78).
Marian Johnson. (Photo: S. Risedorph)

16. FOLK ART BIRD (Pattern #83). Rita Nelson.
(Photo: Barbara Hunt)

17. RUCHED RIBBON ROSE LYRE II (Pattern #70).
Judy DeCosmo. (Photo: S. Risedorph)

18. CORNUCOPIA III (Pattern #71). Jean Wittig.
(Photo: S. Risedorph)

17

18

19. VICTORIAN VASE OF FLOWERS II (No pattern).
Kathryn J. (Joy) B. Jung. (Photo: S. Risedorph)

QUILT #1 THE BALTIMORE BEAUTIES ALBUM.▼

Group quilt made under the author's direction. 95" x 95".
1988–1993. Ruth Meyers hand appliquéd and embroidered
the border, made the center block, and set the quilt together. "Part Three: The Quiltmakers" lists this quilt's
blocks and borders and where you can find these patterns
in the *Baltimore Beauties* series. (Photo: J. Mathieson)

19

20                                                                              21

20. HALF-WREATH OF BLOOMS FROM MRS. MANN'S QUILT (Pattern #80). Herzie Aslankhani. (Photo: S. Risedorph)

21. GERANIUM BIRD (Pattern #79). Marjo Hodges. (Photo: S. Risedorph)

22. ALBUM IN A ROSE LYRE WREATH (Pattern #75). Yvonne Sutton Suutari. (Photo S. Risedorph)

22

QUILT #2 THE NEEDLEARTISTS' ALBUM.

Group quilt under the direction of the author. 68" x 81".
1985–1992. Joy Nichols hand appliquéd and embroidered
the borders and the center medallion. Quilt set together
by Ruth Meyers. Quilted and bound by Joyce Hill. "Part
Three: The Quiltmakers" lists this quilt's individual
patterns and where you can find them in the *Baltimore
Beauties* series. (Photo: J. Mathieson)

23

24

23. VASE OF FULL-BLOWN ROSES II:
ROSE AMPHORA (Pattern #72). Katherine
Kent Ivison Fowle. (Photo: S. Risedorph)

24. THE ALBUM (Pattern #46 in *Baltimore
Album Quilts*). Letty Martin.
(Photo: S. Risedorph)

25. MARYLAND MANOR HOUSE (Pattern #50 in
*Baltimore Album Quilts*). Julie T. Bruss.
(Photo: S. Risedorph)

26. VASE OF FULL-BLOWN ROSES IV (Pattern #29
in *Baltimore Album Quilts*).
Annie Tuley. (Photo: S. Risedorph)

25

26

27

28

**27. LOVE BIRDS ON A ROSE PERCH** (Pattern #81). Barbara Hain. (Photo: S. Risedorph)

**28. STRAWBERRY WREATH III** (Pattern #73). Mary Ann Andrews. (Photo: S. Risedorph)

**QUILT #3. HEART-GARLANDED ALBUM.** ▶

Group Quilt under the direction of the author. Approximately 87" x 87". 1992–93. The women who appliquéd the blocks are listed in "Part Three: The Quiltmakers." Border by Annie Tuley. Quilted by Genevieve A. Greco. Patterns for this entire quilt are in *Design a Baltimore Album Quilt!* While all the blocks in this quilt are hand-appliquéd, Annie Tuley adapted the Rose Vine Border (Pattern #1), curving the vine to facilitate its appliqué by machine. Machine embroidery in wool echoes this design style in antique Baltimores. (Photo: J. Mathieson)

QUILT #4. ALBUM IN HONOR OF MOTHER.

Group top made under the author's direction. 81" x 81". 1990–1992. Central
medallion hand-appliquéd (with dimensional flowers) and embroidered by
Barbara Hahl and Yolanda Tovar. Borders by Ruth Meyers and Sylvia Pickell.
Setting together and the making of the piped and scalloped edging from
*Design a Baltimore Album Quilt!* are by Ruth Meyers. *Baltimore Beauties* series
patterns for these blocks and borders are listed in "Part Three: The
Quiltmakers." (Photo: J. Mathieson )

QUILT #5. ODYSSEY QUILT.

Joy Jung. Approximately 100" x 100".
1989–1994. Joy's son, Matthew Austin
Jung, had his silhouette done in January
1978. He centers both this magnificent
quilt and the odyssey! The quilt includes
both blocks and a border of Joy's design.
(Photo: Richard Pound of Don Pound Studio)

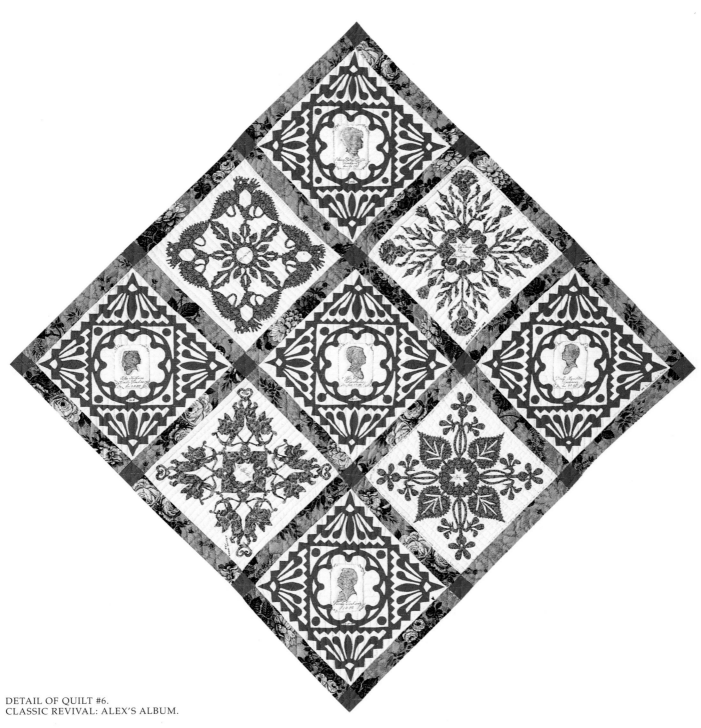

DETAIL OF QUILT #6.
CLASSIC REVIVAL: ALEX'S ALBUM.

Portrait blocks of the author's family form
a medallion and frame Alex Corbly
Sienkiewicz, whom the quilt honors.
Makers of the individual blocks are listed
in "Part Three: The Quiltmakers."
Quilting by Mona Cumberledge.
(Photo: S. Risedorph)

QUILT #6. CLASSIC REVIVAL: ALEX'S ALBUM.

Group Quilt under the author's direction. 96" x 96". 1985–1991. Borders by
Nonna Crook and Albertine Veenstra. Setting together by Carol Elliott. Design,
fabric choice, pattern-drafting and inkwork by the author. Quilting by Mona
Cumberledge. The border's initials, A.C.S., are those of the author's middle
child, Alex, for whom the quilt was made. Patterns for this quilt's papercut
blocks are in this book. (Photo: S. Risedorph)

◄ DETAIL OF QUILT #7. FRIENDSHIP'S OFFERING.

▼ DETAIL OF QUILT #7. FRIENDSHIP'S OFFERING.

QUILT #7. FRIENDSHIP'S OFFERING.

(First pictured in *Baltimore Beauties and Beyond, Vol. I.*) Group Quilt made for Mary Sue Hannan's 70th birthday. 115" x 115". 1986–1988. Makers of individual blocks and the quilt's inscription are listed in *Volume I.* Center medallion by Kate Fowle; quilting brokered by Georgiana B. Fries of Bellwether Dry Goods, Lothian, Maryland. Patterns for this quilt's papercut blocks are in this book. (Photo: Gary E. Garrison)

QUILT #8. BALTIMORE-STYLE ALBUM.

Gerry Sweem. 78½" x 78½". February 1991 to January 1992. Block C-2 is Gerry's original design. The border is reverse-appliquéd. Its pattern was taken from a traditional quilt stencil, which was redrawn. This quilt won Viewers' Choice and Chairman's Choice Awards at San Fernando Valley Quilt Association Quilt Faire in 1992 and represented the Valley Quiltmakers' Guild at the Pacific International Quilt Festival in San Francisco in 1992. (Photo: G. Sweem)

QUILT #9. LOOK WHAT HAPPENED
ON MY WAY TO BALTIMORE!

Laura Reif Lipski. 82" x 82". June 1990 to June
1991. Laura writes that "this quilt was inspired by
pictures of old Baltimore Album Quilts, Elly
Sienkiewicz's books and articles in *Quilter's
Newsletter Magazine,* and a workshop with her at
Long Island Quilters' Society in March 1990—as
well as other books and magazine articles." What
a glorious quilt!  (Photo: Dan Howell for *Quilt!)*

29

30

31

29. ALBUM BLOCK CASE (Closed for carrying. Directions in Appendix II). JoAnne Cardone Maddalena. (Photo: S. Risedorph)

30. ALBUM BLOCK CASE (Open. Directions in Appendix II). JoAnne Cardone Maddalena. (Photo: S. Risedorph)

31. BLOOMS BEYOND BALTIMORE (No pattern). Original design by Jane Townwick showing exceptional fabric use. Well-grounded in the classic tradition, Jane's work is self-confident and boldly original. With JoAnne's carrying case and Jane's beautifully "Beyond Baltimore" block, we close this unit of the Color Section! (Photo: Mitch Mandel)

# PAPERCUT BLOCKS, BORDERS AND ALBUMS

QUILT #10. BALTIMORE-STYLE ALBUM. ▶

Suzanne (Sue) W. Linker. Approximately 55" x 55". 1989–1992. Sue designed this quilt's sashing and borders, observing that "cutwork borders make wonderful frames." (Photo: S. Risedorph)

QUILT #11. LINDSAY'S ALBUM. ▼

Kathryn Blomgren Campbell for her daughter, Lindsay Kathryn (born 8/7/74). 95" x 95". February 1988 to December 1989. Most of this quilt's papercut blocks have full patterns in this volume. The border pattern is in *Appliqué 12 Borders and Medallions!* (Photo: Barbara Hunt)

◀ QUILT #12. REMEMBRANCE.

Jan Sheridan. 47" x 47". 1988. Happy family memories are sure to wrap Jan's daughter, Anne, for whom this quilt was made. (Photo: Anne Sheridan)

▼ QUILT #13. REMBRANCE II.

Jan Sheridan. 50" x 50". 1988. A sister Papercut Family Album reflects fond remembrances for Jan's daughter Kathryn Elizabeth Sheridan. (Photo: A. Sheridan)

QUILT #14. FLOWER DANCERS. ▶

Papercut designed by Sara Harwin. 28" x 28".
1991. Appliquéd and quilted by Sharon Singer.
(Photo: Courtesy of Sara Harwin)

QUILT #15. BONNIE'S ALBUM. ▼

Kathryn Blomgren Campbell for her daughter,
Bonnie Elizabeth (born 3/25/77). 86" x 103".
February 1988 to December 1989. Most of this
quilt's papercut blocks have full patterns in this
volume. The border pattern is in *Appliqué 12
Borders and Medallions!* (Photo: B. Hunt)

32

32. TIPTOE THROUGH MY TULIPS (Pattern #69). Gwendolyn LeLacheur. (Photo: S. Risedorph)

▼QUILT #16. SNOWFLAKES FOR LINDSEY.

Original design by Virginia Ferrill Piland. 96" x 108". 1981. The Album's snowflakes are appliquéd and quilted with trapunto. The diamond-shaped quilting pattern frames other "snowflakes" in the print of the fabric. The border was designed to compliment the field of snowflakes. (Photo: Albert Mooney)

PART THREE:

# THE QUILTMAKERS

About the Needleartists whose work appears in *Papercuts and Plenty: Volume III of Baltimore Beauties and Beyond*—When a quiltmaker contributes stitchery, or a photo to the *Baltimore Beauties* series, she fills out a short questionnaire. The following brief biographies are taken from material thus provided. *Note:* Biographical notes on needleartists generally appear only once in the series even though their work may appear in several volumes. To record who made which blocks in Classic Revival: Alex's Album, a credit line—but no biography—is listed when a needleartist has appeared previously in this series (or where we have lost touch over the years and my inquiries have been "returned to sender"). Some of these needleartists are professionals, and many offered their stitching talents as gifts after we had met just briefly in a class. For some, it was long ago, now. I've been further privileged to correspond with and to see some numbers of you again, over the years. The "quilting world" has become very much a real community where we can hope to meet again at a class or at a quilt show or at a convention. These *Baltimore Beauties* books, then, have themselves become veritable "Friendship Albums," and for that I thank you, each and every one.

MARY ANN ANDREWS of La Canada, California: Strawberry Wreath III.

"After 15 years of quilting I find that I have more and more ideas that just must become quilts. I love small take-along projects especially ones tiny enough and lightweight enough to take backpacking. I love to sit on a rock amid wildflowers high above the tree line in the Sierra Nevadas and merrily stitch away."

HERZIE ASLANKHANI of Castro Valley, California: Half-Wreath of Blooms from Mrs. Mann's Quilt.

"I am interested in all kinds of crafts. My mother taught me knitting and embroidery at the age of 7. I love counted cross-stitch, and 'tagging.' Have been quilting for about 19 years and four years ago fell in love with appliqué and do it most of my time each day."

LEONA BALOG of Hillman, Michigan: Heart-Garlanded Album Block.

"My first quilt was done 53 years ago. I lived in Michigan and my grandmother in Ohio. She sent me the pattern and instructions. Any questions, I just wrote and asked her. I milked cows for 50 years and am now enjoying the free time with quilting. I especially like the challenge of appliqué."

GINNI BERG of Milpitas, California: Red Bird on a Passion Flower Perch.

"I came to quilting in 1976 when I joined the Santa Clara Valley Quilt Association after moving to the Bay Area. I got into teaching...[through] a local craft shop...and have had a lot of enjoyment from teaching. I have worked for an aerospace company as a technical illustrator and over the years have gone through the ranks of Graphic Artist and Commercial Artist...[to doing] most of my work in computer graphics. In the last few years I have wandered off to join a couple of other guilds in addition to SCVQA. In my spare time I also work in 1" scale miniatures, both dolls, houses, and vignettes."

CATHERINE A. BERRY of North Quincy, Massachusetts: Fleur-de-Lis, One-half, and One-quarter Edging Blocks (Classic Revival: Alex's Album).

CAROL ANN BLANK of Milwaukee, Wisconsin: Heart-Garlanded Album Block.

"I've been quilting for 11 years and been a member of the Wisconsin Quilters [for most of that time]. ...Making quilts, cross-stitching, and making dolls is very fulfilling for me. I also enjoy doing commission work for others, too. ...I've been very lucky with the support and understanding of my family for the long hours I put into my quilting and other interests. ...I put my whole heart into everything I do, and I'm very proud of my work."

JO ANN CRISMON BOWMAN of San Antonio, Texas: Heart-Garlanded Album Block.

"My mother taught me at a young age to sew, embroider, crochet, and when 11 years old, I helped her quilt. I made my first baby quilt in 1943 when 14 for my youngest brother born of six children. When the San Antonio Quilt Guild was formed in 1980, I was inspired by other quilters, learned better quilting techniques, and have received awards in our quilt shows."

KATHLEEN BRASSFIELD of Prairie Village, Kansas: Christmas Cactus (Classic Revival: Alex's Album).

JANE BRAVERMAN of Prairie Village, Kansas: Turtle Hill and Botanical Variation (Classic Revival: Alex's Album).

"I prefer the precision and geometry of piecing, but admire the freedom appliqué allows a designer/quilter. My work is influenced by Jinny Beyer and Roberta Horton. I live in Prairie Village with husband David, daughters Rebecca and Erica, dog Muffin, and cats Crystal and Clea."

MARIAN K. BROCKSCHMIDT of Springfield, Illinois: Palmetto Medallion (Classic Revival: Alex's Album).

JEANNE BRONIKOWSKI of Milwaukee, Wisconsin: Heart-Garlanded Album Block.

"Wife, mother, grandmother with a degree in Occupational Therapy and Art, Jeanne learned the needlearts from her mother when very young. She has been teaching quilting and other needlearts for more than 20 years. She is a member of the Wisconsin Quilters and other local guilds. She has published two pattern books through her business, Quilting Arts."

HELEN M. BROOKS of North Syracuse, New York: Hearts and Tulips (Classic Revival: Alex's Album).

"Married with four children, the love of sewing was very beneficial. Began teaching in 1979, offering a beginner's quilt class in her home. From this class she founded the Plank Road Quilt Guild in 1980. She has taught quilting classes in quilt shops and with guilds."

JULIE T. BRUSS of Green Bay, Wisconsin: Maryland Manor House.

"I have two children, a husband and a full-time job. Quilting is a way of life for me. I love the challenge and creativeness of Baltimore Album quilts. I would like to be remembered by my family and friends by the quilts and blocks I've made."

MARION E. BURKE of Oak Bluffs, Massachusetts: Heart-Garlanded Album Block.

"Some of my fondest childhood memories are of summers in Prince Edward Island, Canada. My cousins and I would share secrets late into the night under quilts they had made with my aunts and grandmother. We could pick out scraps from last year's school dress, a special party dress, or a favorite blouse. For me, quilts, whether traditional or contemporary, are stories and memories."

DIANE CAPITANI of Wilmette, Illinois: Sunburst Medallion with Fleur-de-Lis (Classic Revival: Alex's Album).

"Grandmother was [of] Mennonite origin. She and her oldest daughter quilted extensively. My mother did not, so I came to quilting 15 years ago when [my] first daughter was born. I've taught, lectured—love all handwork, including cross-stitch, needlepoint, embroidery, knitting. I was one of the founders of the Illinois Quilters Guild."

LINDA CARLSON of Orchard Heights, Missouri: Heart-Garlanded Album Block.

"I have been quilting since the late '70s. Recently, I finished a research paper on large, four-block quilts, pieced or appliquéd. My next goal is to write a book on these quilts. I was a co-founder of the Prairie Pine Quilt Guild in Mexico, Missouri, and I also served on the Missouri State Quilter's Guild Board of Directors."

NAN CARTER of Vineyard Haven, Massachusetts: Heart-Garlanded Album Block.

"I'm a transplant from New Jersey where I taught quiltmaking for the Embroiderers' Guild and at the Arts Workshop of the Newark Museum and studied color theory and design. ...I started out as an embroiderer, picked up needlepoint and weaving on the way, and find myself happiest with a thimble and a quilting needle in my hand."

GEORGIA CIBUL of Wilmette, Illinois: Fleur-de-Lis and Laurel Sprays (Classic Revival: Alex's Album).

DONNA COLLINS of Bridgeport, New York: Palmetto Medallion (Classic Revival: Alex's Album).

PATRICIA NOEL CONNET of La Cygne, Kansas: Palmetto Medallion (Classic Revival: Alex's Album).

"A registered nurse, married with three grown children, who is enjoying working part-time and pursuing a hobby she loves, quilting. As a child she remembers her mother and the neighbor ladies getting together for quilting bees in the quiet rural setting of La Cygne. She particularly likes to appliqué and has a quilting business on the side. She loves to get together with her quilting friends to share enthusiasm and ideas."

SHERRY COOK of Emporia, Kansas: Heart-Garlanded Album Block.

"I was taught to quilt by my grandmother at the age of 5, but my serious interest was renewed in 1982. I am active in my local quilt guild and have finished my second term as President of the Kansas Quilters' Organization. I was an accountant for the Emporia State University Endowment Association for a number of years but currently devote all my time to quiltmaking."

JOSEPHINE ANN COON of Clay, New York: Hearts and Pinecones for Maine, One-half, and One-quarter Edging Blocks (Classic Revival: Alex's Album).

"Born and raised in Central, New York. Married with two children. Love for needle and thread started at the age of 9. I always had the appetite to explore and do something different. Needlework is my relaxation, my sanctuary from everyday routine. [For] seven years I...owned a quilt shop and have been teaching quilting and stenciling. Though I do all types of quilting, I'm partial to appliqué."

NONNA CROOK of Gallup, New Mexico: Two borders (Classic Revival: Alex's Album).

JUDY DeCOSMO of Grosse Point Woods, Michigan: Ruched Ribbon Rose Lyre II.

"I love appliqué. I chose a Baltimore Album style wall hanging to do for our 1988 Quilt Challenge for the Quilt Guild of Metro Detroit. It contained over 400 pieces within its 22" x 22" size. I used the freezer paper technique, and it turned out so well, I won the contest. Thank you for teaching me."

ETHEL DEVILLEZ of Buzzards Bay, Maine: Heart-Garlanded Album Block.

"I have owned Quilts-n-Things, Ltd., along with my sister, Pat, and cousin, Debbie, for four years. I started appliquéing with an Appliqué Sampler, continued to Country Bride, then Pennsylvania Bride, and am now on my Baltimore Album. Love to appliqué and quilt!"

JOY EATON of Sugar Creek, Missouri: Ring with Holly (Classic Revival: Alex's Album).

"I enjoy quilting mostly for [my] daughters and grandaughters. Like all kinds of

hobbies and crafts (smocking). Started quilting from Dee Thomas in 1973."

CAROL ELLIOTT of Washington, D. C.: Setting together of Classic Revival: Alex's Album

Years before the author started to quilt, Carol Elliott, her neighbor, was the neighborhood quiltmaker. Carol is a school dietitian who after hours does gourmet cooking, quilting, dressmaking, and a seemingly endless array of handwork as it catches her fancy!

JOAN C. ENNIS of Northfield, Minnesota: Heart-Garlanded Album Block.

"I am working professionally as the reference librarian in the Northfield Public Library. I am also a writer and have had stories published for children. I have always been interested in needlework and began sewing and needlework projects as a child. I have made many quilts, have taught quilting, and have won ribbons at the Minnesota State Fair. Baltimore Album quilts suit my love of appliqué and handwork."

KATHARINE KENT IVISON FOWLE of Washington, D. C.: Epergne of Fruit III; Vase of Full-Blown Roses II: Rose Amphora.

Since Kate's work first appeared in *Volume I*, she has gone on to become a highly esteemed jeweler whose work is sold widely. In addition, she teaches those aspects of her craft, including beadmaking, which she has refined. We're sorry to lose you from quiltmaking, Kate, but congratulate you on your stellar achievements as a jeweler!

WENDY J. GRANDE of Aptos, California: Epergne of Fruit IV.

"I have always enjoyed the opportunity for expression that quilting provides with color, form, and texture. I am inspired by all around me, my family, our vacations, and the work of other quilters. It is important to preserve needlework—knitting, crochet, tatting, ribbonwork, and fine hand sewing. However, I always come home to quilting." Wendy has been the author's invaluable Teaching Assistant once a year at California's Asilomar Quilt Conference for a number of years. In addition to her remarkable needleartistry, she is the mother of two and a high-powered banking executive.

LEE GRAVINA of Bradenton, Florida, and Sandwich, Massachusetts: Heart-Garlanded Album Block.

"Sewing for my four children, home, and myself for many years was my way of relaxing. However, shortly after my first quilt was completed, I knew that I had found a love for quiltmaking. I have been quilting and teaching others what I know for 18 years. Appliqué quilts are my sole interest, and I have found great pleasure and fulfillment in teaching others what I love to do so much."

GENEVIEVE A. GRECO of Murrysville, Pennsylvania: Quilting design and stitching of Heart-Garlanded Album Quilt.

"Gen is a wife and mother of three with a grand passion for hand quilting. She has taught quilting since 1987, currently instructing beginning and advanced students at Calico Hearts in Penn Hills, Pennsylvania. Her 'Through Rose-Colored Stitches' won an honorable mention in Chitra Publications 'Miniatures from the Heart' contest, which was recently on tour. She has quilted for private collectors across the United States."

ROSIE GRINSTEAD of Mission Hills, Kansas: Grandma's Scottish Thistle (Classic Revival: Alex's Album).

"I come from a family of quiltmakers and seamstresses, so learned to sew very early in my life. I've always been involved in handicrafts, but didn't start quilting until the mid-1970s. Then I was making small boutique items, but I soon got hooked on quilts. I've made baby quilts for friends and family and many, many wall hangings, but few large quilts. One of my large quilts, Kansas Medallion, won the Kansas Quilt Contest in 1987."

BARBARA J. HAIN of Spokane, Washington: Lovebirds in a Rose Perch.

"I began quilting in 1982, and from the onset have had a real love for the patterns, textures, and colors that are a part of the 'Art of Quilting.' In the beginning, it was piecing that fueled my enjoyment, but in the last several years I have challenged myself with traditional appliqué in order to expand my horizons and grow as a quilter. Beside quilting itself, I am involved in my local quilt guild and do civic work in my community. I am also an architect." Secretly, Barbara organized her Asilomar class to make an Album of Double Heart blocks for the author, their teacher. What a wonderful gift from all of them!

SUE HALE of Upland, California: Promises (Baltimore Album Picture block in *Appliqué 12 Easy Ways!*).

"My interest in quilts began with the gift of a beautiful Log Cabin quilt made from the dark silk wedding dresses of my great-grandmother and great-aunts. Quiltmaking, handweaving, rugmaking, sketching, and photography were my favorite avocations during the years I taught English, raised two sons, and completed a Master's degree. Now 'retired' from the aerospace industry, I'm devoting all of my time to appliqué and design."

SARA HARWIN of Portland, Oregon: Flower Dancers (designed by Sara).

"Her work begins with an idea that has developed over a period of time. The spark may have been a holiday, a life celebration, a costume, or just a pose. A recurring motif in Sara's work is the dance. 'It has been a form of celebration since the beginning of time. It flows in wonder and awe, taking on different forms yet still always the same,' she explains. Folk, ballet, and jazz elements vitalize her artwork."

DIXIE HAYWOOD of Pensacola, Florida: *Scherenschnitte* Heart.

"I've loved fabric and the threaded needle since my mother taught me to sew in grade school, but I always claimed I didn't think in appliqué—until I got an idea that could only be done with appliqué. [I've] been quilting steadily since the 1960s; also enjoy teaching, writing, designing, and judging."

REGINA H. HELFER of Deerfield, Illinois: Pinks / Carnations (Classic Revival: Alex's Album).

"I took my first quilting class six years after the birth of my son. I needed a creative outlet, and quilting filled that need. I've been quilting ever since, mostly for family and friends and occasionally for a local craft show. Of all the different quilt techniques, hand appliqué is my favorite."

JOYCE HILL of Bens Run, West Virginia. Needleartist's Album.

"A native West Virginian, Joyce learned to quilt at a young age. Her first attempt at quilting was creating quilts for the birth of her first child. She is the mother of two children: Jason, age 12, and Heidi, age 18. Joyce keeps a quilt in the frame all the time. She is employed by H&R Block from January through April and spends the remainder of the year sewing and quilting."

NANCY HORNBACK of Wichita, Kansas: Palmetto Medallion (Classic Revival: Alex's Album).

EVA L. HUDSON of Lawrence, Kansas: Devon Violets for Grandma (Classic Revival: Alex's Album)

"I began making doll clothes on my grandmother's treadle machine at the age of 5, and I've never stopped sewing. I soon began piecing quilts and quilting with my mother and grandmother. I have always loved sewing. I have sewn professionally (making costumes, draperies and clothing). In 1977, I joined Kaw Valley Quilters Guild of Lawrence, Kansas, and have taken all the workshops offered there from many quilt artists. I have worked at the University of Kansas Museum of Natural History for 28 years and am planning to retire...to devote more time to quilting."

SHIRLEE HUGGER of Oak Bluffs, Massachusetts: Heart-Garlanded Album Block.

Shirlee is an enthusiastic appliquér, making beautiful blocks for herself and others. She even took her quiltmaking to sea, joining the author on a Caribbean cruise in 1993.

MARIAN JOHNSON of Campbell, California. Basket of Full-Blown Roses.

"I lived on a farm in South Dakota during the '20s and '30s, learning needlework from my mother. I do all kinds of sewing, made my children's clothes, and still make my own. My greatest love now is quilting, attending seminars and classes frequently. I just finished an heirloom quality quilt for my daughter, named "Wreath of Flowers," my own design, all appliqué. Now retired in Northern California, I belong to a quilt association, and am a Board Member of The American Museum of Quilts and Textiles in San José. I staff, am a docent, do outreach programs, and other activities. Always busy!"

DONNA JO JONES of St. Charles, Missouri: Landon Bears and One-quarter Block (Classic Revival: Alex's Album).

"Quilting for me began as a sampler class and a way to get back in the real world after my daughter started first grade. I've tried most every type of needlework, but piecing and quilting seemed to be exactly what I had been searching for. Soon all other projects were relegated to the back of the closet, and I was doing consignment work for the local quilt shop. I joined Little Hills Quilt Club and was Vice President-Program Chairman. ...My hands are busy with my quilting, and my mind is busy with new ideas."

KATHERYN J. (JOY) B. JUNG of Granville, Ohio: Victorian Vase of Flowers II, Odyssey Quilt.

"Joy began quilting in 1978. Her true growth came after a move to Phoenix, Arizona, in 1987. She was strongly influenced by classes with Elly Sienkiewicz and Laurene Sinema. Her love of old designs and quilts has only increased since her family moved back to Ohio."

YVONNE KASPER-HOGAN of Chicago, Illinois: Heart-Garlanded Album Block.

Yvonne is an avid quilter and a member of Illinois Quilters, Inc. Yvonne, who is self-taught, began quilting only a few years ago.

LOIS KAVANAGH of Edgartown, Massachusetts: Heart-Garlanded Album Block.

"For this amateur, the needlearts provide a medium for communication and interaction. I value the opportunity to clarify thinking as well as improve skill—to remember that this is my joy."

LISA ANNE LANDRY of Pelham, New Hampshire: Heart-Garlanded Album Block.

"Taught needlearts as a small child by her mom and grandmothers, Lisa pursued a career in quilting when retiring (very young) from L&O/NICU nursing. She has won many blue ribbons at state fairs. Her quilts grace the walls of office buildings in New England. Her latest commissioned work is 48 quilts of various sizes for the Children's Hospital at Dartmouth Hitchcock Medical Center in Lebanon, New Hampshire. ...Lisa's love of quilting shows in all her work."

LAURA REIF LIPSKI of Lindenhurst, New York: Look What Happened on My Way to Baltimore!

On her needleartist form, Laura wrote this most gracious note: "Elly, Thank you for this honor. You wrote in my book, 'who will surely take Baltimore beautifully "beyond."' Perhaps you write that in all, but I was touched, and I hope you feel I've gone part of the way. You've made me proud of my work. ...Quilting continues to challenge me, to satisfy my creative needs, to keep me company, and help me encourage others and myself to fight low self-esteem, to give me purpose and direction."

MARGIE LOFTHUS of Fairway, Kansas: Botanical Variation and One-half Block (Classic Revival: Alex's Album).

"I have been doing needlework since I was 4 and must say it is one of the most joyful experiences of my life. I can cry at the sight of a beautiful quilt. I feel great kinship with women of yesterday and today who can create such art and evoke such emotion with little scraps of cloth, often the things that others throw away."

JO ANNE CARDONE MADDALENA of Coram, Long Island, New York: Album Block Case.

"Sewing has always brought me pleasure. As early as age 5 or 6, I was making doll clothes, crocheting, or trying embroidery. One of my favorite memories is of being taught to use my grandmother's treadle sewing machine. ...I have always made clothing for myself and my five children. It was when my youngest child entered kindergarten in 1982 that I found time to investigate quilting. I quickly discovered 'what I want to do when I grow up.'"

LETTY MARTIN of Troy, Michigan: The Album.

"Letty has been sewing since the age of 5. Her love of art and color has found its expression in quilts. She has been making quilts and teaching quilting since the early 1980s. While enjoying all aspects of quilting, recent work in appliqué has led to a particular interest in those old quilts appliquéd using the straight stitch on the sewing machine. Working to develop techniques, which allow today's quilters to successfully machine appliqué, has been a rewarding part of her teaching."

KAY MAYHEW of Vineyard Haven, Massachusetts: Heart-Garlanded Album Block.

"I taught a Baltimore Album quilt class, and it made me proud that three of my students also made squares for this quilt. When my first quilt won a ribbon from the National Quilting Association in 1974, I knew I had found an activity I would enjoy for the rest of my life. Although I prefer appliqué, I have made more than 100 pieced quilts. Probably

because I am also a genealogist, I treasure old quilts."

RUTH H. MEYERS of Dharan, Saudi Arabia, and Exmore, Virginia: Borders and setting-together of the Baltimore Beauties Album; one and a half borders, the setting-together, and the piped and scalloped edging of Album in Honor of Mother.

The Gulf War occurred during the time Ruth worked on the Baltimore Beauties Quilt borders. On August 28, 1991, she wrote: "There wasn't really anything special working on this border. I just had to put it down more often and scramble to the 'safe room.' When we heard the sirens, we dropped everything and went to our 'secure' area. Since there are no bomb shelters in Saudi Arabia, we were instructed to provide a safe room within our houses. We taped windows and air-conditioning vents, stockpiled food and water. We equipped the room with TV, radio, and telephone; gas masks were ready. My husband sandbagged the outside wall. Most of the alerts were in the evening or during the night, and we had made our bedroom the designated area. Most of the time, we just turned over and went back to sleep. There was nothing gained by getting excited.

"Everyday life just about came to a standstill, so I had lots of time to work. One eye on the TV, one ear listening for sirens, and every 15 minutes a take-off of four to six fighters from the adjacent air base 'somewhere in the eastern Province' drowning out everything.

"We made it, and the memory is already fading. ...Enclosed is a clip from our local newspaper. I thought this could have come from a memorial block of a Baltimore Album Quilt." Ruth's clipping pictured an aviator-helmeted young man and carried this verse, "In Memory / If tears could build a stairway / And heartaches make a lane / We would walk the path to heaven / And bring you home again." It was signed "Missed very much, His Family." Ruth's Quilt, Baltimore Beauties for Bob, won "Best of Show by Hand" at C&T Publishing's Baltimore Album Revival Contest in Lancaster, Pennsylvania, April 1994. The color photo of this prizewinning quilt appears in *Stitched in Cloth, Carved in Stone*.

MARY WISE MILLER of Raytown, Missouri: Palmetto Medallion featured on this book's cover (Classic Revival: Alex's Album).

ARLENE NABOR of Bartlett, Illinois: Cherubs (Classic Revival: Alex's Album).

"I come from a quilting family. My Great-Aunt Kate was a professional quilter. She had her frame attached to the ceiling by ropes. My sister and I always thought this was our playhouse. It was a good way to stay out of the way. I'm 57-years-old [she wrote when she stitched her block] and love quilting. It's a good way to be frugal. I prefer appliqué to patchwork, but love them both. My fabric collection rivals a fabric shop in quantity. It also covers fabrics from the 1920s to the present. I also collect books and patterns regarding quilting."

RITA NELSON of Washington, D. C.: Folk Art Bird.

"I have been involved with handcrafts since the age of 5 when my grandmother taught me to crochet. Quilting is a...passion, which began...years ago when the neighborhood Murch Quilters asked me to join their group. Now there is always a quilting project in process, such as the rain forest theme quilt I [worked] on for the National Zoo in Washington. What a wonderful way to spend leisure time!"

ELLEN NEUBER of Falmouth, Massachusetts: Heart-Garlanded Album Block

"I began quilting about 10 years ago, have gone through many stages, have learned from many great teachers, and am now enjoying putting my own techniques and ideas into my own [work]. I've found from Baltimore blocks a whole different kind of quilting and designing on my own."

BRENDA PAPADAKIS of Indianapolis, Indiana: George Washington's Redbud (Classic Revival: Alex's Album).

VIRGINIA FERRILL PILAND of Berea, Kentucky: Snowflakes for Lindsey.

"My work, with the exception of only a few exploratory attempts at piecing, is appliqué and embroidery. 'Snowflakes' is an early work (1981) in which I conformed to the format and size of the traditional quilt. ...This quilt was made for my daughter Lindsey. The snowflake design was chosen to represent her individuality."

LINDA L. PLYLER of Mason, Missouri: Heart-Garlanded Album Block.

"Linda is a quilter with varying interests.

...Her appliqué work ranges from child-like folk art to very fine detail work. When working with Baltimore-style blocks, she is very traditional, but when she teaches Baltimore style, she encourages experimentation with color—using color as the outlet for creativity while using traditional patterns and techniques."

HILLA PRIDDY of Belleville, Indiana: Oak Leaves and Acorns (Classic Revival: Alex's Album).

GERRI RATHBUN of Independence, Missouri: Rose Medallion (Classic Revival: Alex's Album).

BILLYE M. REYNOLDS of Cedar Hill, Texas: Heart-Garlanded Album Block.

"I have been sewing all my life and teaching sewing a good deal of my adult life. ...Although I'm new to the appliqué technique used in Album quilts, I find it especially restful somehow to think of the links the design I'm stitching could have to the past. The history of quilts and quilting keeps creating new challenges for me."

MARY JO RIDGE of Medford, Massachusetts: Alex's Cats, One-half and One-quarter Blocks (Classic Revival: Alex's Album).

"One of the more vivid memories of my childhood is the day my mom taught me how to thread a needle and sew. I made many doll clothes. My love for stitching was renewed after I married in 1985 and observed my mother-in-law's needleart. My first completed piece was a small wall hanging entitled 'A Geologist's Grand Canyon' drafted by my husband, Jack. (We are both geologists.) I am actively involved with local quilt groups and hope to eventually teach [quilting]."

NANCY MATHIESON RIECK of Crystal Lake, Illinois: Flowers Around Friendship's Chain.

"Nancy's interest in clothing and its construction began in her childhood. ...She earned a certificate in fashion merchandising from the Ray School of Design and worked in the field for five years. Family work in the Scottish needleart of embroidery inspired her interest and work in traditional embroidery, crewel, and needlepoint. In 1972, she inherited family tops from the 1930s, which were influenced by the Century of Progress Fair in Chicago, and she began learning how to complete them. The discovery that quilting brings together all of her interests in textiles, design, pattern construction, and history is providing wonderful opportunities to study and socialize as well as to create."

VIRGINIA ROBERTSON of Overbrook, Kansas: Botanical Variation: Red-Blossomed Sprays.

"Owner of the Osage County Quilt Factory publishing business with her husband, Virginia is the designer of patterns for quilt and fabric crafts. She has two art degrees and a background as an art professor at three universities, worked as a display and fabric department manager for department stores, and has 15 years of quilting experience. The Quilt Factory patterns and books are distributed nationwide. Virginia's husband, Lyn, runs the business end and keeps track of over 15,000 retail and wholesale accounts."

KAYE SCHNELL of Falmouth, Massachusetts: Heart-Garlanded Album Block.

"I have a degree in Business Administration, worked as an administrative assistant in the legal field and taught needleart when I retired. Quilting is a personal love that has turned into a new career. I've been teaching quilting since 1975. My three children have homes of their own, and my husband understands my passion for quilting, so I have time to indulge myself."

LESLIE SHAW of Gillette, New Jersey: Heart-Garlanded Album Block.

"I have always loved doing things with my hands. I left my job as a buyer for Macy's after my oldest daughter Kate was born. I happened upon a quilting class at the local adult school and was fascinated by the entire process. Appliqué instantly became my favorite type of quilting, and the Baltimores have been an inspiration."

JAN SHERIDAN of Spruce Head, Maine: Album Quilts, Remembrance I and Remembrance II; top border and drafting of medallions in Friendship's Offering.

Jan brings both artistry and a draftsman's knowledge to quilting. She and the author met while working on "Friendship's Offering" for mutual friend, Mary Sue Hannan. Inspired by that project, Jan went on to stitch youthful memories into Papercut Albums for each of her daughters.

SHARON SINGER of Portland, Oregon: Flower Dancers (appliquéd and quilted by Sharon).

Sharon and her sister-in-law, Sara Harwin, have collaborated on other quilts of Sara's design. To Sara's designs, Sharon brings an enthusiastic and skillful quiltmaker's talents. The teamwork results in quite wonderful works of art!

ELEANOR (HONEY) COLLIMORE SLUBEN of Meredith, New Hampshire: Heart-Garlanded Album Block.

"When my husband Dick and I decided to move to New Hampshire in 1987, I envisioned mountains of snow, crackling fires, learning to quilt, and putting up blueberries. As it turned out, I'm so busy with quilting, I haven't had time for the blueberries. At first, I hated appliqué because everyone in my 'block of the month class' groaned when the 'A' word was mentioned and because I didn't know that with good teachers, tools, techniques, and time, my fascination would blossom."

LINDA BARCELO STIPEK of Montgomery, Massachusetts: Heart-Garlanded Album Block.

"I studied at the Boston Museum School of Fine Arts. Now that my four children are grown, I have time to devote to the art of quiltmaking. Now I'm free to study color, form, [and] design, and experience the pure joy of creating in fabric. There is a grand sense of peace working with a needle. I feel a bond with quiltmakers of the past and a oneness with today's quilters."

YVONNE SUTTON SUUTARI of Boynton Beach, Florida: Album in a Rose Lyre Wreath.

"Ever since I can remember, I have always been interested in any form of needleart and sewing from dressmaking, knitting, crochet, needlepoint, crewel to embroidery and cross-stitch. Then, about 11 years ago, while working in Saudi Arabia, I met a group of American ladies who introduced me to the delights of quilting through a Cathedral Window pillow. Since that time, I have been addicted and haven't stopped learning as many new techniques as possible. My particular love is embroidery and appliqué. Over the years I have made a number of quilts, but now my main interest is in Baltimore Album quilts. I am an active member of the Boynton Beach Library Quilters, the Delray Quilters, Crazy Quilters of Lake Worth, and the Gold Coast Quilters' Guild. I also work part-time and have a very active little boy, but I still manage to find time most days to do a little quilting."

GERRY SWEEM of Reseda, California. Baltimore-Style Album.

"This quilt is a result of a workshop with Elly where I learned the cutwork technique. This quilt won Viewers' Choice and Chairman's Choice Awards at the San Fernando Valley Quilt Association Quilt Faire in 1992 and represented Valley Quiltmakers' Guild at the Pacific International Quilt Festival in San Francisco in 1992."

ANNE TEDROW of Rantoul, Illinois: Heart-Garlanded Album Block.

"Quilting is the 'piece' in my life. As the wife of an Air Force officer, it has been my privilege to travel many places and meet many people. I have quilted with the Amish in Delaware, appliquéd a Baltimore Album quilt in Austin, Texas, taken classes in Houston and Paducah, and this all happened in the last few years. Everywhere we move, my icebreaker in a room full of strangers, has been 'Does anyone quilt?' It works everytime! I haven't met a quilter I didn't like."

DEOLINDA THOMAS of Independence, Missouri: Sunflower (Classic Revival: Alex's Album).

"Being a self-taught traditional quilter, I most enjoy reproducing old quilt blocks or the entire quilt. When I see something I really like, I have to have it right now. ...It was a real thrill when I purchased an old torn quilt at a flea market for $7.50 and now have a new, beautiful reproduction of it."

JANE TOWNSWICK of Schnecksville, Pennsylvania: Blooms Beyond Baltimore.

"Jane is a quilter and former shop owner, and is now an editor at Rodale Press. Her first love is appliqué, followed by hand quilting, knitting, crochet, needlepoint, and tatting. She has written Classic Country Quilts with the editors of Quilter's Newsletter Magazine, published by Rodale Press, and Quiltmaking Tips and Techniques, published by Rodale Press." Jane is well on her way to two Albums. Her blocks are so unique and beautiful that one is shown here in the Color Section for inspiration.

ANNIE T. TULEY of Export, Pennsylvania: Border of Heart-Garlanded Album (Classic Revival: Alex's Album).

ALBERTINE VEENSTRA of Acton, Massachusetts: Palmetto Frame, two full borders;

helped two other needleartists by finishing the Pineapple block and two Botanical Variation half blocks (Classic Revival: Alex's Album).

SHIRLEY C. WEDD of Lawrence, Kansas: E Pluribus Unum: Eagles and Oaks (Classic Revival: Alex's Album).

"I made quilts for my daughter and son when they moved from the crib to a youth bed. I knew nothing about quilting at that time. I became interested in quilting again about 1977 and took a week of classes and from then on I have been quilting and taking workshops to help me keep learning. My daughter, Shirlene Wedd, is also a quilter, and we often work together on many projects."

MARY WHEATLEY of Mashpee, Massachusetts: Heart-Garlanded Album Block.

"I cannot recall a time in my life when my leisure hours were not spent doing some form of needlework or other handwork. Researching the history and varied methods, and acquiring a high level of skill in my work has always been important to me. ...A Hawaiian quilt made for my daughter turned me onto appliqué, which is now one of my favorite techniques."

ALICE L. WILHOIT of Anna, Texas: Heart-Garlanded Album Block.

Alice is the Director of Education at Sharon's Quilt Depot in McKinney, Texas (near Dallas). She says, "quilts have been an important part of my life. My earliest memories include nights when I would snuggle down into my grandmother's feather mattress with the weight of her quilts on me and days when I would play under her frame as she and her friends would quilt. I began quilting in the mid-1980s and am now busy building memories for my grandchildren."

JEAN G. WITTIG of Washington, D. C.: Cornucopia III.

"A special education teacher and now a librarian with the D. C. Public Schools for the past 20 years, I have been quilting for the past 17. It's a good thing I started when I did, or I might never have started as my son and daughter, twins, were born the next year. Since then, I have been involved in several quilting groups including one I started, which has made 10 quilts to benefit my children's elementary school. While I love all kinds of quilts, I particularly enjoy making portrait quilts of my family."

BETTY YOUNG of Mashpee, Massachusetts: Heart-Garlanded Album Block.

"I have been sewing since I can remember. I started quilting in 1976 while working in a fabric store. When moving to the Cape in 1986, there was more time to spend quilting. I have made quilts for my six children, and started a Baltimore Album in May 1992."

DEBRA BOTELHO ZEIDA of Waquoit, Massachusetts: Heart-Garlanded Album Block.

"Debbie first fell in love with quilting in 1977 when she and her husband honeymooned in beautiful Lancaster County, Pennsylvania. They bought their first quilt, a Bridal Wreath, from a very dear Amish lady, Mrs. Jonas Good. Ten years later, Debbie took her first quilting class. She hasn't stopped since. Mother of a busy teenager, Debbie is always working on an appliqué project at Rob's baseball games or play rehearsals."

## ABOUT THE MAKERS OF THE *BALTIMORE BEAUTIES* SERIES GROUP ALBUM QUILTS IN THE COLOR SECTION

The needleartists who created the **Album in Honor of Mother (Quilt #4 in the Color Section)** follow. The name of the book where each block pattern can be found is in parentheses.

A-1 Elly Sienkiewicz (*Dimensional Appliqué*); A-2 Debbie Ballard (*Dimensional Appliqué*); A-3 Roslyn Kempston (*Dimensional Appliqué*); A-4 Marjorie Kruty (*Volume I, Pattern Companion*); B-1 Marjo Hodges (*Dimensional Appliqué*); B-2 (center medallion) Barbara Hahl and Yolanda Tovar (*Appliqué 12 Borders and Medallions!*); B-4 Letty Martin (*Volume I, Pattern Companion*); C-1 Annette Mahon (*Volume I, Pattern Companion*); C-4 Elizabeth Anne Taylor (*Dimensional Appliqué*); D-1 Barbara Hain (*Volume III*); D-2 Elly Sienkiewicz (*Dimensional Appliqué*); D-3 Annie Tuley (*Volume III*); D-4 Elly Sienkiewicz (*Volume I, Pattern Companion*); Sylvia Pickell and Ruth H. Meyers reverse appliquéd the borders. Ruth Meyers set the quilt together and added the piped and scalloped edging from *Design a Baltimore Album Quilt!* Both the central medallion and the border pattern are in *Appliqué 12 Borders and Medallions!*

The needleartists who made **The Needleartists'**

**Album (Quilt #2 in the Color Section)** follow. The name of the book where each block pattern can be found is in parentheses.

Block A-1 Mary Ann Andrews (*Volume III*); A-2 Wendy Grande (*Dimensional Appliqué*); A-3 Stell Lundergren (*Volume I*); A-4 Marjo Hodges (*Volume III*); A-5 Mary Lou Fox (*Volume I*); Block B -1: Donna French Collins (*Volume II*); Center Medallion: Joy Nichols (*Appliqué 12 Borders and Medallions!*); B-4 Julie T. Bruss (*Volume I, Pattern Companion*); B-5 Sue Linker (*Volume I, Pattern Companion*); C-1 Sylvia Pickell (*Volume I, Pattern Companion*); C-4 Donna French Collins (*Volume II*); C-5 Herzie Aslankhani (*Volume III*); D-1 T. A. Peters (*Volume I*); D-2 Dot Reise (*Volume I*); D-3 Yvonne Sutton Suutari (*Volume III*); D-4 Rita Nelson (*Volume III*); D-5 Roberta H. Floyd (*Volume I*); Border and center medallion by Joy Nichols. Border and center medallion patterns are both in *Appliqué 12 Borders and Medallions! — Patterns from Easy to Heirloom.* Set together by Ruth H. Meyers; quilted by Joyce Hill.

The needleartists who created the **Baltimore Beauties Album Quilt (Quilt #1 in the Color Section)** follow. The name of the book where the block pattern can be found is in parentheses.

A-1, Ginni Berg (*Volume I*); A-2 Julie Hart (*Volume II*); A-3 Maxine Satchell (*Volume I, Pattern Companion*); A-4 Georgia Cibul (*Volume I, Pattern Companion*); A-5 Jean Wittig (*Volume III*); B-1 Joy Nichols (*Spoken Without A Word*); B-2 Doris Seeley (*Volume I*); B-3 Jeannie Austin (*Volume I, Pattern Companion*); B-4 Georgeanna Clark (*Volume I, Pattern Companion*); B-5 Judy DeCosmo (*Volume III*); C-1 Gene Way (*Volume I*); C-2 Catherine Berry (*Volume I*); C-3 Ruth Meyers (*Volume I, Pattern Companion*); C-4 Kathryn J.B. Jung (*Volume III*); C-5 Sallye Sileski (*Volume I*); D-1 Joy Nichols (*Volume I*); D-2 Eleanor Kay Green Hunziger (*Volume I, Pattern Companion*); D-3 Kate Fowle (*Volume III*); D-4 Gerri Rathbun (*Volume I, Pattern Companion*); D-5 Elly Sienkiewicz (*Volume I*); E-1 Jerre Reese (*Volume I, Pattern Companion*); E-2 Marian Johnson (*Volume III*); E-3 Donna Teague Scranton (*Volume I, Pattern Companion*); Rose Vine Border (*Appliqué 12 Borders and Medallions!*); setting together by Ruth H. Meyers; quilting by Mona Cumberledge.

The needleartists who made blocks for the **Heart-Garlanded Album (Quilt #3 in the Color Section)** follow.

All the patterns, both for each block and

for the border of this quilt are in *Design a Baltimore Album Quilt!* Leona Knorr Balog, Carol Ann Blank, JoAnn Crismon Bowman, Jeanne Bronikowski, Marion E. Burke, Linda Carlson, Nan Carter, Sherry Cook, Ethel Devillez, Joan Ennis, Lee Gravina, Regina H. Helfer, Yvonne Hogan with Annie Tuley, Shirlee Hugger, Lois Kavanagh, Lisa Landry, Kay Mayhew, Ellen Neuber, Linda Plyler, Gerri Rathbun, Billye M. Reynolds, Kaye Schnell, Leslie Shaw, Linda Stipek, Eleanor Sluben, Anne Tedrow, Betty Young, Mary Wheatley, Alice Wilhoit, and Debra Botelho Zeida. The machine-appliquéd, wool-embroidered border was made by Annie Tuley. Annie adapted the original's somewhat angular border design to one more easily done by machine. The quilting design and its stitching is by Genevieve Greco.

The needleartists who made **Classic Revival: Alex's Album (Quilt #6 in the Color Section)** follow.

Catherine A. Berry, Kathleen Brassfield, Jane Braverman, Marian K. Brockschmidt, Helen M. Brooks, Diane Capitani, Donna Collins, Patricia Noel Connet, Josephine Ann Coon, Joy Eaton, Rosie Grinstead, Regina H. Helfer, Nancy Hornback, Eva L. Hudson, Donna Jo Jones, Margie Loftus, Mary Wise Miller, Arlene Nabor, Brenda Papadakis, Hilla Priddy, Gerri Rathbun, Mary Jo Ridge, Nancy Mathieson Rieck, Virginia Robertson, Deolinda Thomas, Albertine Veenstra, and Shirley C. Wedd. Two borders were appliquéd by Nonna Crook and two borders by Albertine Veenstra. The author chose the colors, drafted the patterns, made kits and inked the blocks after they were appliquéd. Carol Elliott sewed the quilt together; Mona Cumberledge quilted it. The block patterns for this quilt are here in *Volume III.* The border pattern is in *Appliqué 12 Borders and Medallions!*

**Friendship's Offering (Quilt #7 in the Color Section)** group quilt made for Mary Sue Hannan's 70th birthday, 1986-88. 115" x 115". Makers of individual blocks and the quilt's inscription are listed in "Part Three: The Quiltmakers" page 109, *Volume I.* Center medallion by Kate Fowle; quilting brokered by Georgiana Fries, 1988.

# PART FOUR:
# THE PATTERNS

The patterns that follow are given on one-half, one, two, and four pages. The pattern transfer method depends on the number of pages and is explained in detail in *Volume I's* Part One: Getting Started. The pattern names, when given, are ones that I have created, since no original printed source for the old patterns is known. If a block is taken from a Baltimore Album Quilt, its style is labeled Classic Baltimore. If the style looks like mid-19th-century Baltimore, but the provenance is uncertain, its style is called Baltimore-Style.

And if a pattern's style is beyond Baltimore in time or space, it carries the notation, Beyond Baltimore. The symbolic meanings are taken from my first book on the Albums, *Spoken Without A Word*.

Patterns #1 through #69 are papercut blocks designed by a folded, then cut, paper pattern. A favorite way to sew these is by cut-away appliqué with freezer paper on the top (Lesson 2 in *Volume I*). Because technique preferences differ from one quiltmaker to another, one or more of the appliqué methods taught in *Volume I* is suggested for each pattern. The papercut blocks fill an 11½" square design image area: smaller than the 12½" format *Baltimore Beauties* have hitherto followed. In general, antique Albums made all of papercut motifs had smaller blocks than did Albums where the more complex blocks predominate. However, when you mix these *Volume III* papercut patterns with other blocks in *Spoken Without a Word* and the *Baltimore Beauties* series (all of which are presented at a design image 12½" square), you'll find that they look just fine on that larger 12½" format. If, however, you do your own papercuts to design an original pattern, use an 11½" square to fold or design so that you make patterns consistent in size with these Pattern Section patterns.

**PATTERN #1: One of 32 patterns (Block A-1, Kangaroos) from Friendship's Offering, Quilt #7.**

**Type: Beyond Baltimore.** Designed by the author.

To make this block, refer to *Volume I*, Lesson 1 or 2.

**PATTERN #2: One of 32 patterns (Block A-2) from Friendship's Offering, Quilt #7.**

**Type: Beyond Baltimore**

To make this block, refer to *Volume I*, Lesson 1 or 2.

**PATTERN #3: One of 32 patterns (Block A-3) from Friendship's Offering, Quilt #7.**

**Type: Beyond Baltimore**

To make this block, refer to *Volume I*, Lesson 1 or 2.

**PATTERN #4: One of 32 patterns (Block A-4) from Friendship's Offering, Quilt #7.**

**Type: Beyond Baltimore**

To make this block, refer to *Volume I*, Lesson 1 or 2.

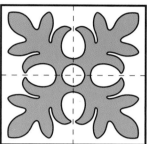

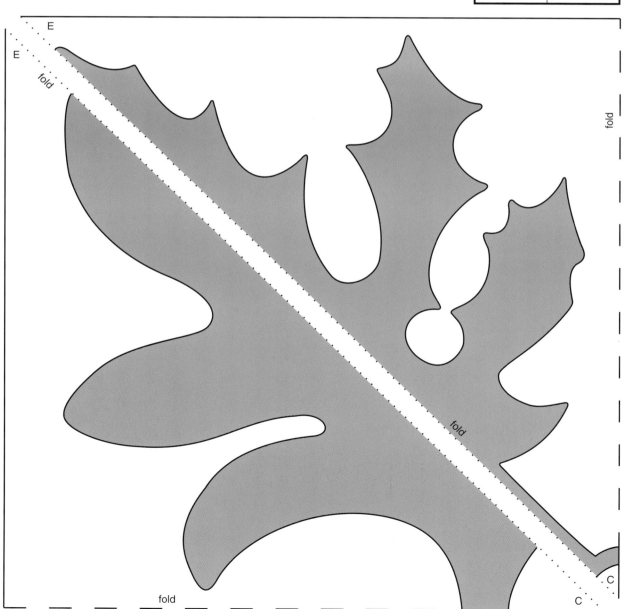

**PATTERN #5: One of 32 patterns (Block A-5) from Friendship's Offering, Quilt #7.**

**Type: Beyond Baltimore**

To make this block, refer to *Volume I*, Lesson 1 or 2.

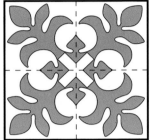

**PATTERN #6: One of 32 patterns (Block A-6) from Friendship's Offering, Quilt #7.**

**Type: Beyond Baltimore**

To make this block, refer to *Volume I*, Lesson 1 or 2

**PATTERN #7: One of 32 patterns (Block B-1) from Friendship's Offering, Quilt #7.**

**Type: Beyond Baltimore**

To make this block, refer to *Volume I*, Lesson 1 or 2.

**PATTERN #8: One of 32 patterns (Block B-2) from Friendship's Offering, Quilt #7.**

**Type: Beyond Baltimore**

To make this block, refer to *Volume I*, Lesson 1 or 2.

**PATTERN #9: One of 32 patterns (Block B-3) from Friendship's Offering, Quilt #7.**

**Type: Beyond Baltimore**

To make this block, refer to *Volume I*, Lesson 1 or 2.

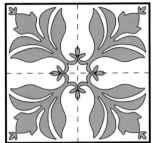

**PATTERN #10: One of 32 patterns (Block B-4) from Friendship's Offering, Quilt #7.**

**Type: Beyond Baltimore**

To make this block, refer to *Volume I*, Lesson 1 or 2.

**PATTERN #11: One of 32 patterns (Block B-5) from Friendship's Offering, Quilt #7.**

**Type: Beyond Baltimore**

To make this block, refer to *Volume I*, Lesson 1 or 2.

**PATTERN #12: One of 32 patterns (Block B-6) from Friendship's Offering, Quilt #7.**

**Type: Beyond Baltimore**

To make this block, refer to *Volume I*, Lesson 1 or 2.

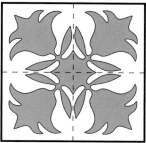

**PATTERN #13: One of 32 patterns (Block C-2, Cabin Fever Calicoes) from Friendship's Offering, Quilt #7.** (*Note:* The next two blocks in Row C, C-3 and C-4, are made from Pattern #38 in *Baltimore Album Quilts, Pattern Companion to Volume I,* as are blocks D-3 and D-4 in Row D.)

**Type: Beyond Baltimore.** Designed by the author.

To make this block, refer to *Volume I*, Lesson 1 or 2. Read Formula #6 (page 52 in this book) to see how this asymetrical pattern was designed. Cut template as a four-repeat pattern.

**PATTERN #14: One of 32 patterns (Block C-5, Hearts and Hands) from Friendship's Offering, Quilt #7.**

**Type: Beyond Baltimore.** Designed by the author.

To make this block, refer to *Volume I*, Lesson 1 or 2. Read Formula #6 (page 52 in this book) to see how this asymetrical pattern was designed. Cut template as a four-repeat pattern.

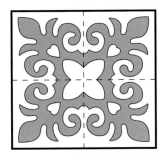

**PATTERN #15: One of 32 patterns (Block C-1) from Friendship's Offering, Quilt #7.**

**Type: Beyond Baltimore**

To make this block, refer to *Volume I*, Lesson 1 or 2.

**PATTERN #16: One of 32 patterns (Block C-6) from Friendship's Offering, Quilt #7.**

**Type: Beyond Baltimore**

To make this block, refer to *Volume I*, Lesson 1 or 2.

**PATTERN #17: One of 32 patterns (Block D-1) from Friendship's Offering, Quilt #7.**

**Type: Beyond Baltimore**

To make this block, refer to *Volume I*, Lesson 1 or 2.

**PATTERN #18: One of 32 patterns (Block D-2) from Friendship's Offering, Quilt #7.** *(Note:* The next two blocks in Row D, D-3 and D-4, are made from Pattern #38 in *Baltimore Album Quilts, Pattern Companion to Volume I.)*

**Type: Beyond Baltimore**

To make this block, refer to *Volume I*, Lesson 1 or 2.

**PATTERN #19: One of 32 patterns (Block D-5, Hearts and Swans) from Friendship's Offering, Quilt #7.**

**Type: Beyond Baltimore.** Contemporary design by Pat Gallagher.

To make this block, refer to *Volume I*, Lesson 1 or 2.

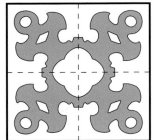

**PATTERN #20: One of 32 patterns (Block D-6) from Friendship's Offering, Quilt #7.**

**Type: Beyond Baltimore**

To make this block, refer to *Volume I*, Lesson 1 or 2.

**PATTERN #21: One of 32 patterns (Block E-1) from Friendship's Offering, Quilt #7.**

**Type: Beyond Baltimore**

To make this block, refer to *Volume I*, Lesson 1 or 2.

**PATTERN #22: One of 32 patterns (Block E-2, Cherubs) from Friendship's Offering, Quilt #7.**

**Type: Beyond Baltimore.** Designed by the author.

To make this block, refer to *Volume I*, Lesson 1 or 2.

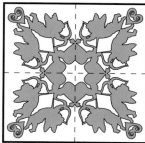

**PATTERN #23: One of 32 patterns (Block E-3) from Friendship's Offering, Quilt #7.**

**Type: Beyond Baltimore**

To make this block, refer to *Volume I*, Lesson 1 or 2.

**PATTERN #24: One of 32 patterns (Block E-4) from Friendship's Offering, Quilt #7.**

**Type: Beyond Baltimore**

To make this block, refer to *Volume I*, Lesson 1 or 2.

**PATTERN #25: One of 32 patterns (Block E-5, Garden Cats) from Friendship's Offering, Quilt #7.**

**Type: Beyond Baltimore.** Designed by the author.

To make this block, refer to *Volume I*, Lesson 1 or 2.

**PATTERN #26: One of 32 patterns (Block E-6) from Friendship's Offering, Quilt #7.**

**Type: Beyond Baltimore**

To make this block, refer to *Volume I*, Lesson 1 or 2.

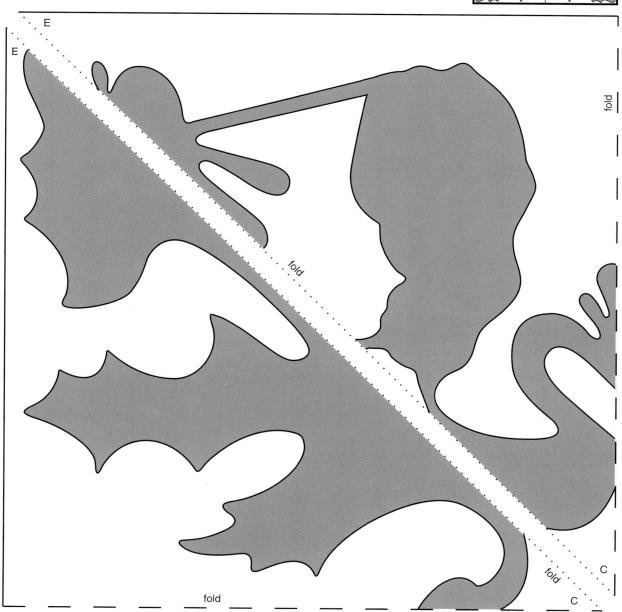

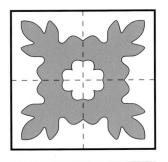

**PATTERN #27: One of 32 patterns (Block F-1) from Friendship's Offering, Quilt #7.**

**Type: Beyond Baltimore.** This is the logo of the Continental Quilting Congress, a contemporary design by Hazel Carter

To make this block, refer to *Volume I*, Lesson 1 or 2.

**PATTERN #28: One of 32 patterns (Block F-2) from Friendship's Offering, Quilt #7.**

**Type: Beyond Baltimore**

To make this block, refer to *Volume I*, Lesson 1 or 2.

**PATTERN #29: One of 32 patterns (Block F-3) from Friendship's Offering, Quilt #7.**

**Type: Beyond Baltimore**

To make this block, refer to *Volume I,* Lesson 1 or 2.

**PATTERN #30: One of 32 patterns (Block F-4) from Friendship's Offering, Quilt #7.**

**Type: Beyond Baltimore**

To make this block, refer to *Volume I,* Lesson 1 or 2.

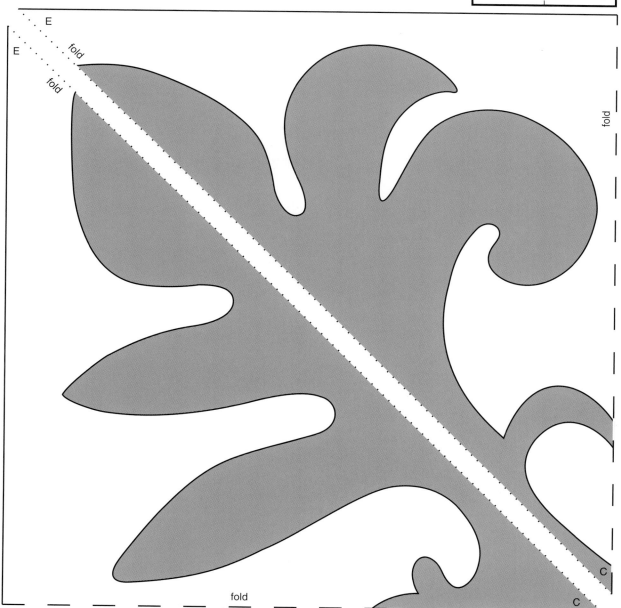

**PATTERN #31: One of 32 patterns (Block F-5) from Friendship's Offering, Quilt #7.**

**Type: Beyond Baltimore**

To make this block, refer to *Volume I*, Lesson 1 or 2.

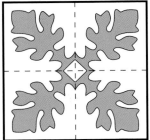

**PATTERN #32: One of 32 patterns (Block F-6) from Friendship's Offering, Quilt #7.**

**Type: Beyond Baltimore**

To make this block, refer to *Volume I*, Lesson 1 or 2.

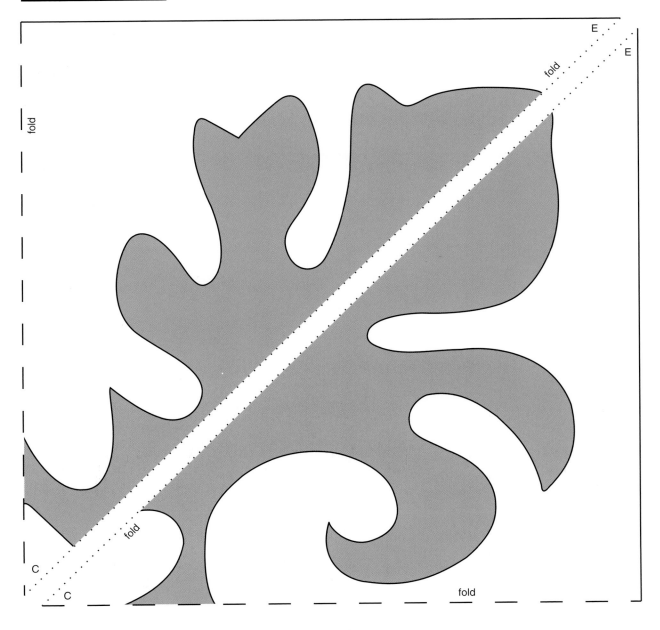

**PATTERN #33: One of 29 patterns (Block A-1, Simpler Palmetto Frame) from Classic Revival: Alex's Album, Quilt #6 in the Color Section.** This pattern occurs in each of that quilt's four corners and in the edging block, E-5.

**Type: Classic Baltimore**

To make this block, refer to *Volume I*, Lesson 1 or 2.

**PATTERN #34: One of 29 patterns (Block A-2, Botanical Variation) from Classic Revival: Alex's Album, Quilt #6.** The next block (A-3) is a variation of Pattern #8 in *Volume I*.

**Type: Baltimore-Style**

To make this block, refer to *Volume I*, Lesson 1 or 2.

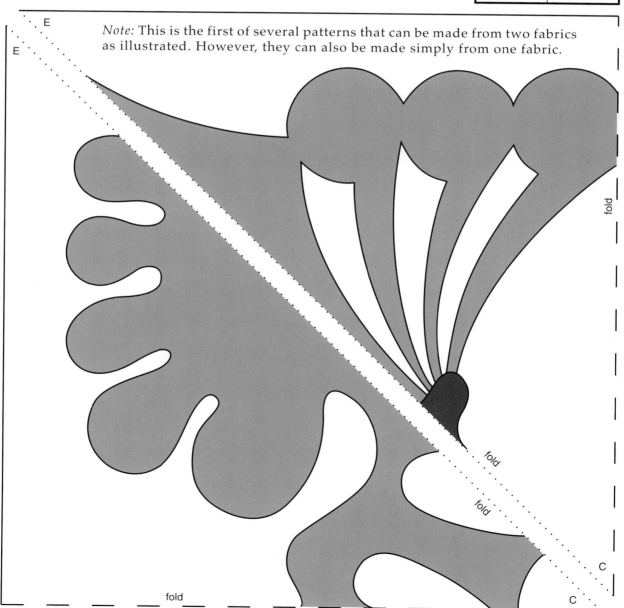

*Note:* This is the first of several patterns that can be made from two fabrics as illustrated. However, they can also be made simply from one fabric.

**PATTERN #35: One of 29 patterns (Block A-4, Pineapple) from Classic Revival: Alex's Album, Quilt #6.** The next block (A-5) repeats Pattern #33.

**Type: Baltimore-Style**

To make this block, refer to *Volume I*, Lesson 1 or 2.

**PATTERN #36: One of 29 patterns (Block B-1, Alex's Cats) from Classic Revival: Alex's Album, Quilt #6.**

**Type: Beyond Baltimore.** Designed by the author. ("A" for Alex sits between these cats.)

To make this block, refer to *Volume I*, Lesson 1 or 2.

**PATTERN #37: One of 29 patterns (Block B-2, Fleur-de-Lis and Rose Medallion) from Classic Revival: Alex's Album, Quilt #6.**

**Type: Beyond Baltimore**

To make this block, refer to *Volume I*, Lesson 1 or 2.

**PATTERN #38: One of 29 patterns (Block B-3, George Washington's Redbud) from Classic Revival: Alex's Album, Quilt #6.**

**Type: Beyond Baltimore.** Designed by the author.

To make this block, refer to *Volume I*, Lesson 1 or 2.

**PATTERN #39: One of 29 patterns (Block B-4, Fleur-de-Lis Variation) from Classic Revival: Alex's Album, Quilt #6.**

**Type: Classic Baltimore, from the Album inscribed "Seidenstricker," "Baltimore," and "1845."**

To make this block, refer to *Volume I*, Lesson 1 or 2.

**PATTERN #40: One of 29 patterns (Block C-1, Botanical Variation) from Classic Revival: Alex's Album, Quilt #6.**

**Type: Classic Baltimore, from the Album inscribed "Seidenstricker," "Baltimore," and "1845."**

To make this block, refer to *Volume I*, Lesson 1 or 2.

**PATTERN #41: One of 29 patterns (Block C-2, Sunflower) from Classic Revival: Alex's Album, Quilt #6.**

**Type: Classic Baltimore, from the Album inscribed "Seidenstricker," "Baltimore," and "1845."**

To make this block, refer to *Volume I*, Lesson 1 or 2.

**PATTERN #42: One of 29 patterns (Block C-3, Palmetto Border) from Classic Revival: Alex's Album, Quilt #6.** This pattern contains silhouette portraits by the author and is repeated in blocks E-2, E-3, E-4, and G-3. The ink portraits were done by Technique #2, which is taught on pages 22–23 in *Volume II*.

**Type: Classic Baltimore, from the Album inscribed "Seidenstricker," "Baltimore," and "1845."**

To make this block, refer to *Volume I*, Lesson 1 or 2.

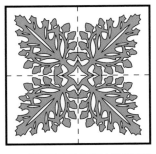

**PATTERN #43: One of 29 patterns (Block C-4, Oak Leaves and Acorns—for Longevity) from Classic Revival: Alex's Album, Quilt #6.**

**Type: Beyond Baltimore.** Designed by the author.

To make this block, refer to *Volume I, Lesson 1 or 2.*

**PATTERN #44: One of 29 patterns (Block C-5, Sweet Gum for the Severn River) from Classic Revival: Alex's Album, Quilt #6.**

**Type: Beyond Baltimore.** Designed by the author.

To make this block, refer to *Volume I, Lesson 1 or 2.*

**PATTERN #45: One of 29 patterns (Block D-1, "Turtle Hill") from Classic Revival: Alex's Album, Quilt #6.**

**Type: Beyond Baltimore.** Designed by the author.

To make this block, refer to *Volume I*, Lesson 1 or 2. Cut the paper template for this block as a four-repeat pattern.

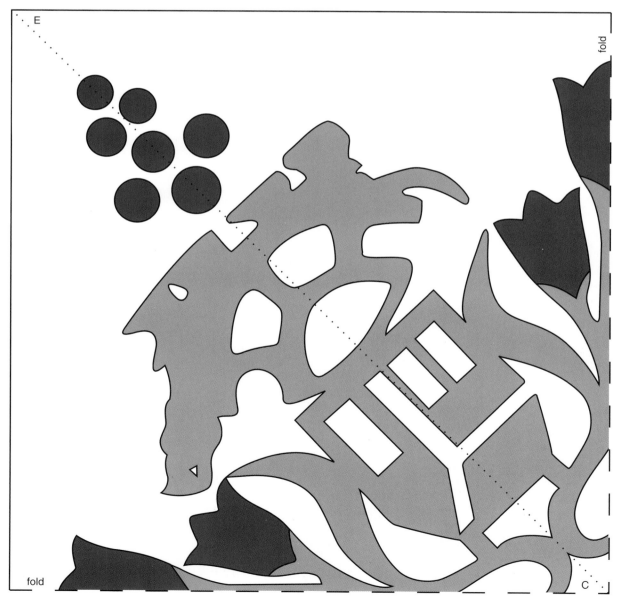

**PATTERN #46: One of 29 patterns (Block D-2, *E Pluribus Unum:* Eagles and Oaks) from Classic Revival: Alex's Album, Quilt #6.** The next block, Block D-3, repeats the Cherubs, Pattern #22 from the quilt, Friendship's Offering.

**Type: Beyond Baltimore.** Designed by the author.

To make this block, refer to *Volume I,* Lesson 1 or 2. For the eagle's feathers, slash to the inside corner's turn line, following the method for Dogtooth Borders taught on page 78 in *Volume II.* Cut the freezer paper template for this pattern as a four-repeat. The shadow box on page 56 explains how this papercut was designed.

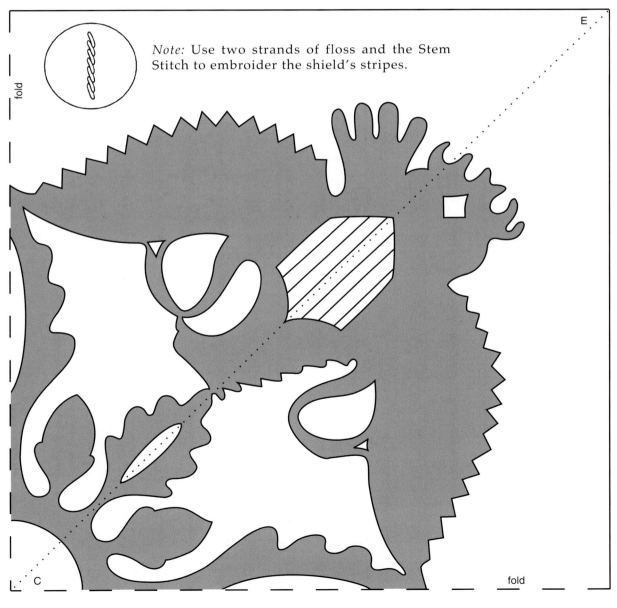

*Note:* Use two strands of floss and the Stem Stitch to embroider the shield's stripes.

**PATTERN #47: One of 29 patterns (Block D-4, Carnations) from Classic Revival: Alex's Album, Quilt #6.**

**Type: Beyond Baltimore.** Designed by the author.

To make this block, refer to *Volume I*, Lesson 1 or 2.

**PATTERN #48: One of 29 patterns (Block E-1, Double Hearts) from Classic Revival: Alex's Album, Quilt #6.**

**Type: Classic Baltimore.** Occurs in the Baltimore Museum of Art's Mary Everist Album among others.

To make this block, refer to *Volume I*, Lesson 1 or 2.

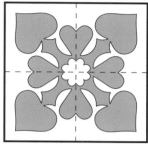

**PATTERN #49: One of 29 patterns (Block F-1, Rose Medallion) from Classic Revival: Alex's Album, Quilt #6.**

**Type: Beyond Baltimore**

To make this block, refer to *Volume I*, Lesson 1 or 2.

**PATTERN #50: One of 29 patterns (Block F-2, Great Grandma May Ross Hamilton's Scottish Thistle) from Classic Revival: Alex's Album, Quilt #6.**

**Type: Beyond Baltimore.** Designed by the author.

To make this block, refer to *Volume I*, Lesson 1 or 2.

**PATTERN #51: One of 29 patterns (Block F-3, Devon Violets for Nana) from Classic Revival: Alex's Album, Quilt #6.**

**Type: Beyond Baltimore.** Designed by the author.

To make this block, refer to *Volume I*, Lesson 1 or 2.

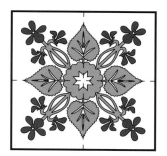

**PATTERN #52: One of 29 patterns (Block F-4, Flowers Around Friendship's Chain) from Classic Revival: Alex's Album, Quilt #6.**

**Type: Beyond Baltimore.** Designed by the author.

To make this block, refer to *Volume I*, Lesson 1 or 2.

**PATTERN #53: One of 29 patterns (Block G-1, Hearts and Tulips) from Classic Revival: Alex's Album, Quilt #6.**

**Type: Classic Baltimore.** From a quilt inscribed with Numsen Family names.

To make this block, refer to *Volume I,* Lesson 1 or 2.

**PATTERN #54: One of 29 patterns (Block G-2, Landon Bears Football Team) from Classic Revival: Alex's Album, Quilt #6.**

**Type: Beyond Baltimore.** Designed by the author.

To make this block, refer to *Volume I,* Lesson 1 or 2. To cut this asymmetrical pattern, refer to Formula #4 on page 51 in this book.

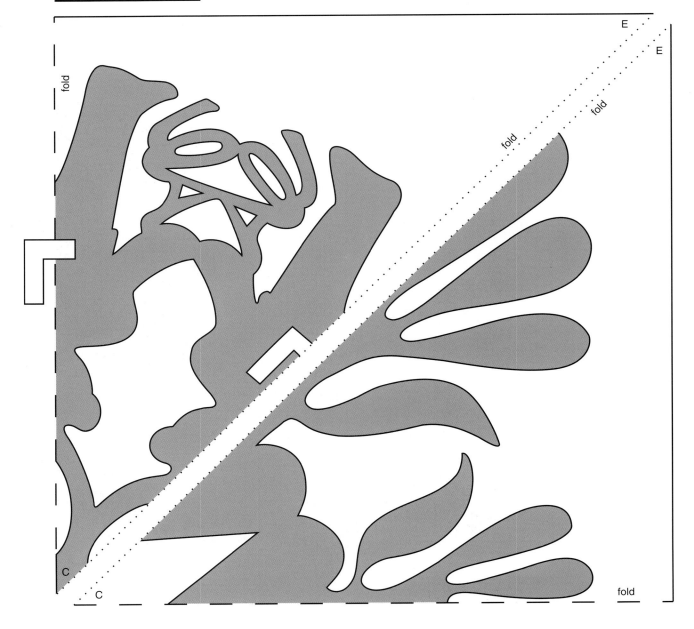

**PATTERN #55: One of 29 patterns (Block G-4, Ring with Holly) from Classic Revival: Alex's Album, Quilt #6.**

**Type: Baltimore-Style**

To make this block, refer to *Volume I*, Lesson 1 or 2.

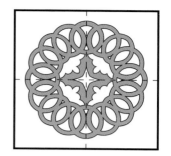

**PATTERN #56: One of 29 patterns (Block G-5, Botanical Variation in Honor of Victoria Jean McKibben Hamilton) from Classic Revival: Alex's Album, Quilt #6.**

**Type: Beyond Baltimore.** Designed by the author.

To make this block, refer to *Volume I*, Lesson 1 or 2.

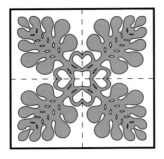

**PATTERN #57: One of 29 patterns (Block H-1, Pinecones for Maine) from Classic Revival: Alex's Album, Quilt #6.**

**Type: Beyond Baltimore.** Designed by the author.

To make this block, refer to *Volume I*, Lesson 1 or 2.

**PATTERN #58: One of 29 patterns (Block H-2, Botanical Variation) from Classic Revival: Alex's Album, Quilt #6.**

**Type: Baltimore-Style**

To make this block, refer to *Volume I*, Lesson 1 or 2.

**PATTERN #59: One of 29 patterns (Block H-3, Christmas Cactus) from Classic Revival: Alex's Album, Quilt #6.**

**Type: Baltimore-Style**

To make this block, refer to *Volume I,* Lesson 1 or 2.

**PATTERN #60: One of 29 patterns (Block H-4, Botanical Variation) from Classic Revival: Alex's Album, Quilt #6.**

**Type: Baltimore-Style**

To make this block, refer to *Volume I,* Lesson 1 or 2.

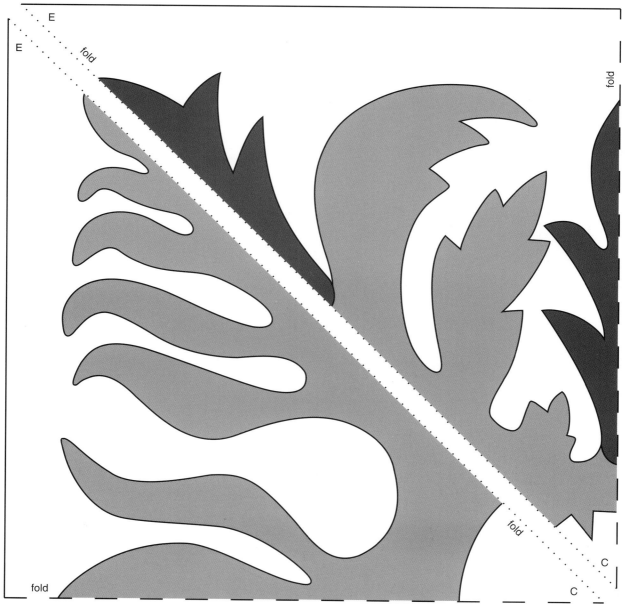

**PATTERN #61: One of 29 patterns (Block I-2, Fleur-de-Lis Variation) from Classic Revival: Alex's Album, Quilt #6.**

**Type: Baltimore-Style**

To make this block, refer to *Volume I, Lesson 1 or 2.*

**PATTERN #62: One of 29 patterns (Block I-4, Fleur-de-Lis Variation) from Classic Revival: Alex's Album, Quilt #6.**

**Type: Classic Baltimore.** From a quilt inscribed "1850."

To make this block, refer to *Volume I, Lesson 1 or 2.*

**PATTERN #63: One of two patterns (Block C-2, Sometimes Take Tea) from Bonnie's Album, Quilt #15.**

**Type: Beyond Baltimore.** Designed by Kathryn Blomgren Campbell.

To make this block, refer to *Volume I*, Lesson 1 or 2. On the pattern, remove the spout from the left side of each teapot at the dashed lines.

**PATTERN #64: One of two patterns (Block B-3, Violins and Bows) from Bonnie's Album, Quilt #15.**

**Type: Beyond Baltimore.** Designed by Kathryn Blomgren Campbell.

To make this block, refer to *Volume I*, Lesson 1 or 2.

**PATTERN #65: One of two patterns (Block D-1, Flamingos) from Lindsay's Album, Quilt #11.**

**Type: Beyond Baltimore.** Designed by Kathryn Blomgren Campbell.

To make this block, refer to *Volume I*, Lesson 1 or 2.

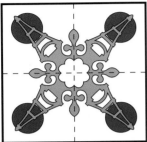

**PATTERN #66: One of three patterns (Block D-3, Eiffel Tower) from Lindsay's Album, Quilt #11.**

**Type: Beyond Baltimore.** Designed by Kathryn Blomgren Campbell.

To make this block, refer to *Volume I*, Lesson 1 or 2.

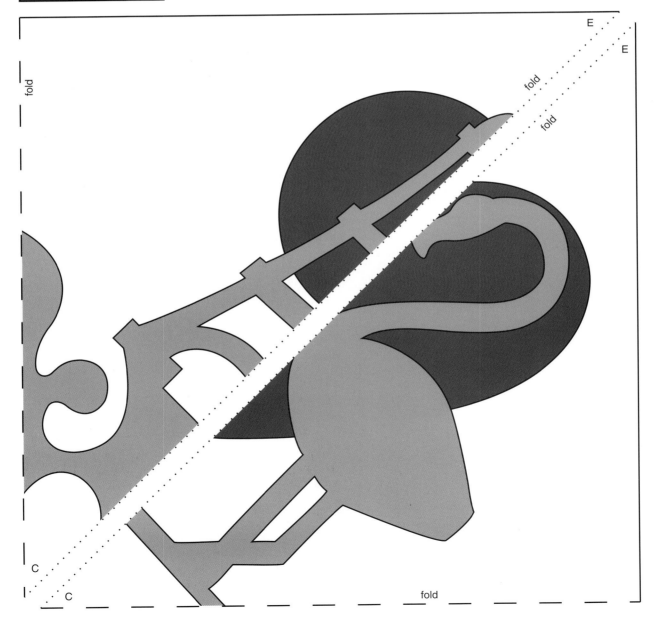

**PATTERN #67: One of three patterns (Block F-2, Lindsay as a Young Gymnast) from Lindsay's Album, Quilt #11.**

**Type: Beyond Baltimore.** Designed by Kathryn Blomgren Campbell.

To make this block, refer to *Volume I*, Lesson 1 or 2.

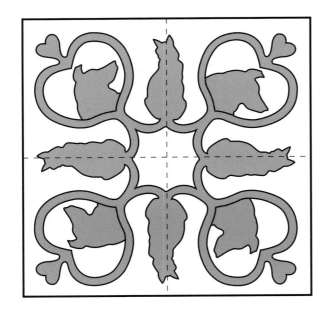

**PATTERN #68: One pattern (Block A-3, Family Pets) from Remembrance II, Quilt #13.**

**Type: Beyond Baltimore.** Designed by Jan Sheridan.

To make this block, refer to *Volume I*, Lesson 1 or 2. Cut four cat and dog templates to tape to the full-size freezer paper pattern. Place these so that all the dogs face clockwise and all the cats face counter-clockwise.

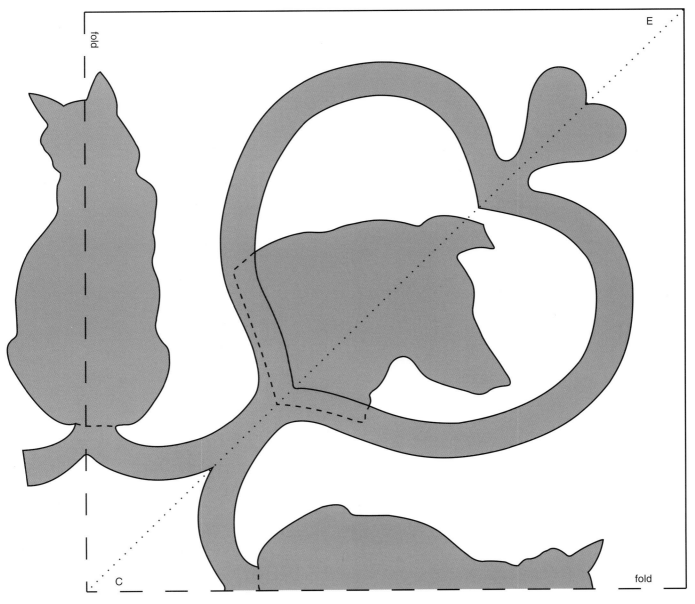

**PATTERN #69: Tiptoe Through My Tulips**

**Type: Beyond Baltimore.** Designed by Gwendolyn LeLacheur.

To make this block, refer to Lessons 3 and 8; in *Volume I*, Lessons 5 and 10. This is a variation of blocks A-3 and I-3 in Quilt #6.

Reminiscent of classic Baltimore, this is a simpler block, which would liven any Album. Gwen used the superfine stem method for the tulip stems, chain-stitch (with two strands of embroidery floss) for the berry stems, and needleturn with freezer paper on the top for both the center frame and the floral appliqués. The center space is just waiting for a benevolent inscription!

Detail of Chain Stitch

fold

fold

E

C

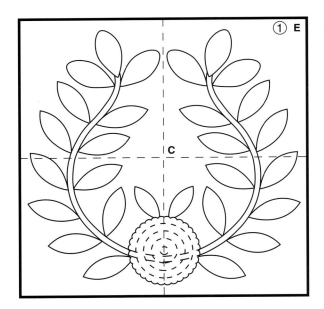

## PATTERN #70: Ruched Ribbon Rose Lyre II

### Type: Beyond Baltimore

To make this block, refer to Lesson 4; in *Volume I*, Lessons 2, 5, 8, 9, and 10.

Pattern from a mid-19th-century Pennsylvania Album. The pattern Ruched Rose Lyre is included in *Volume I*. There, it bears a note saying that I had seen a similar block pictured in a quilt, but having been unable to relocate the photo, I'd recreated that *Volume I* pattern from memory. This second version is a faithful pattern of the antique original pictured in Jane Kolter's *Forget Me Not*. Judy DeCosmo has interpreted the ruching in picot-edged satin ribbon on a spray of country-fresh green geometric cottons. Many such antique Album lyre wreaths are tipped by three red leaves on either side. Were they meant to be rosebuds? Or if the wreath is of

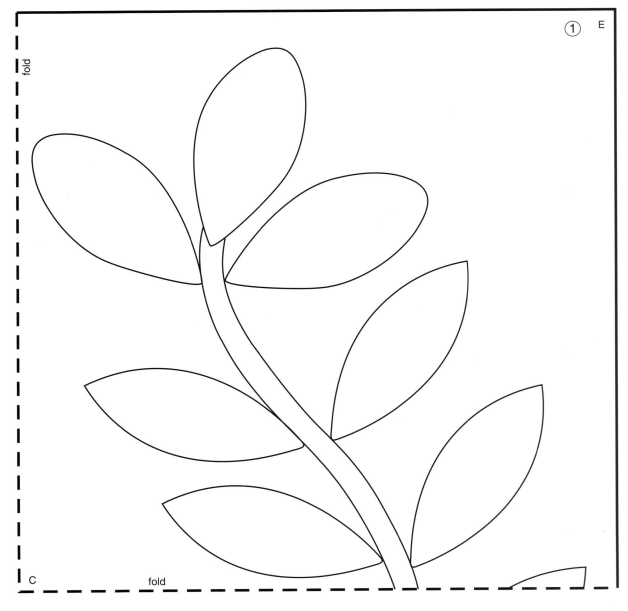

## PATTERN #70: Ruched Ribbon Rose Lyre II

### Second page

laurel, could the laurel be wound with roses and buds? The Victorians made an art of mourning the dead. Their culture of piety included repeatedly stitching, carving, and painting eulogies. One can read signs of *memento mori* in the Album wreaths—whether these be floral wreaths, or heart wreaths and lyre wreaths twined with buds, fruits, and blossoms. Contemporary attitudes toward the dead have differed dramatically from those of Victorian times, but one senses a swing back to those Victorian sensibilities. Then, too, these laudatory wreath symbols can also be sewn for the living who will surely appreciate the approbation!

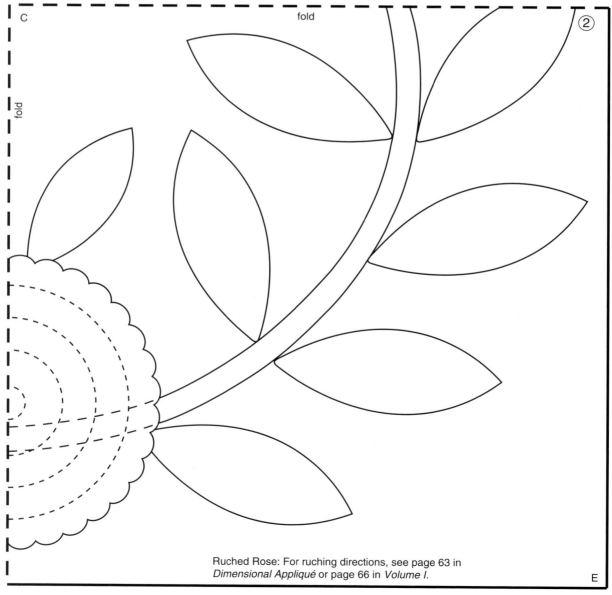

Ruched Rose: For ruching directions, see page 63 in *Dimensional Appliqué* or page 66 in *Volume I.*

**PATTERN #71: Cornucopia III.**

**Type: Classic Baltimore**

To make this block, refer in *Volume I*, to Lessons 2 and 10.

In *Design a Baltimore Album Quilt!* we studied how the appliqué design's shape on a given block can actually help organize the allover interior pattern of an Album Quilt. Blocks set on the diagonal are very useful in this regard, but patterns for them are hard to find. This diagonally placed cornucopia is based on Block E-4 in Ladies of Baltimore, Quilt #4 in *Baltimore Album Quilts, The Pattern Companion to Volume I*. An exceptional

**PATTERN #71: Cornucopia III.**

**Second page**

quiltmaker, Jean Wittig, personalized the pattern a bit by reversing a "W" for her surname into her contemporary reproduction of this block. See color plate 18. Note that this pattern can be oriented on the block to suit your quilt's needs.

**PATTERN #71: Cornucopia III.**

**Third page**

**PATTERN #71: Cornucopia III.**

**Fourth page**

**PATTERN #72: Vase of Full-Blown Roses II: Rose Amphora.**

**Type: Baltimore-Style**

To make this block, refer in *Volume I,* to Lesson 10.

This faithfully reproduced block was first pictured as Color Plate #1 in *Volume I,* but no pattern accompanied it there. Here is the pattern, beautifully interpreted by Kate Fowle. She used multiple commercially dyed reds and whites. The slightly varied dye-lots give depth and richness to the roses. Skillfully, she combined both sophisticated prints and homey calicoes, taking her cues from a photo of the an-

*Note:* This pattern's embroidery is optional. The leaves can be stitched with a single strand of machine embroidery thread using the Stem or Outline Stitch (see page 118). The rose moss can be embroidered in the Fly stitch (see page 59 in *Volume I*) with a single strand of silk sewing thread. These embellishment details can also be drawn with a Pigma pen.

**PATTERN #72: Vase of Full-Blown Roses II: Rose Amphora.**

**Second page**

tique original. This is an exquisite block, one which, once prepared, is neither difficult nor particularly time-consuming to sew. With the exception of the stems, Kate prepared all of her appliqué shapes with the Freezer Paper Inside method. After completing the appliqué, she trimmed away the background cloth (to within ¼" of the seam line) to remove the paper. This lovely piece now hangs in her home, bordered by a Chinese Red sponge-painted wooden frame, which Kate also made.

**PATTERN #72: Vase of Full-Blown Roses II: Rose Amphora.**

**Third page**

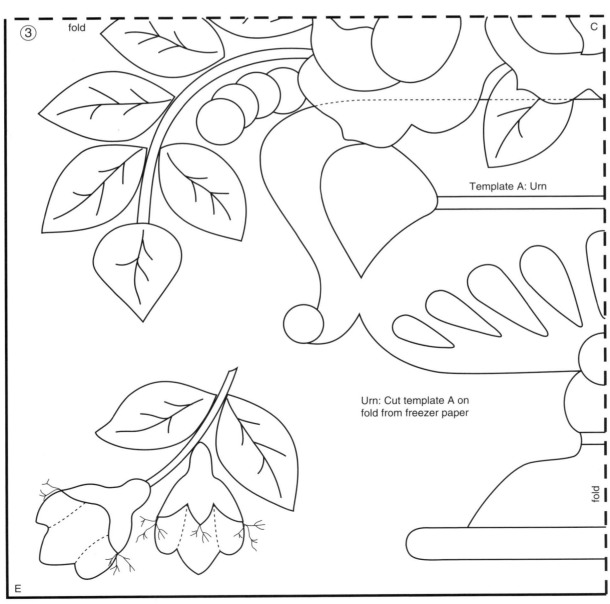

Template A: Urn

Urn: Cut template A on
fold from freezer paper

**PATTERN #72: Vase of Full-Blown Roses II: Rose Amphora.**

**Fourth page**

## PATTERN #73: Strawberry Wreath III.

### Type: Classic Baltimore

To make this block, refer to *Volume I*, Lessons 5, 7, 9, or 10.

Strawberries, meaning "esteem and love," are twined in a circular wreath, framing, in the prototype block, an ardent dedication. Mary Ann Andrews stitched these fruit into fresh abundance with DMC Medici® wool. This block's original is E-2 in Quilt #3 in *Baltimore Album Quilts, A Pattern Companion to Volume I*. Penned carefully in its center is:

## PATTERN #73: Strawberry Wreath III.

### Second page

To the Gray Boys,
Guardians of Freedom, Justice and Virtue
    Citizens, soldiers of Liberty's soil,
This token of Friendship I gladly present you,
    Then guard it from insult and shield it from spoil
Strong be the links in the chain of your union,
    And never the soldiers's proud precept forsake;
Long may you live in a martial communion;
    And scorned be the coward who the conflict sent back.
—M. A. B.
(Transcription from Dunton's *Old Quilts*, page 23. Dena
Katzenberg's *Baltimore Album Quilts*, page 84, transcribes
the last line as "And scorn'd be the slavery who the com-
pact would break.")

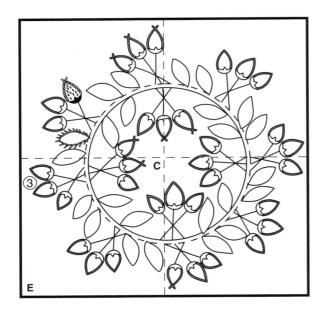

## PATTERN #73: Strawberry Wreath III.

### Third page

*Errata*: In the *Pattern Companion's* Color Section, I mistakenly placed the Gray Boys' inscription in Block C-2, a wreath of roses, rather than its actual location, Block E-2, the Strawberry Wreath. William Rush Dunton, Jr., also suggests in *Old Quilts* (page 23) that "this probably refers to the Independent Grays, a militia company organized in 1787, which...was formed into the Fifth Regiment by an act of 1792. The companies kept their names until the Civil War." In my Album research, I've never come across another reference to the Independent Grays, though Francis F. Beirne in *The Amiable Baltimoreans* (page 95) refers to the Fifth Regiment in Baltimore's War of 1812 victories. He also mentions Baltimore's crack cavalry, the "Independent Blues," in an 1815 civic rite involving plans for Baltimore's Battle Monument (completed in 1825).

Given the considerably later 1840s to 1850s dates on the Album Quilts, I wonder if that verse refers instead to the New Orleans Grays, defenders of the Alamo, heroes whose valiant deeds would recently (May 23, 1846) have been replayed for the Album makers by Sam Houston's crowd-raising oratory on Monument Square. He entreatied Baltimoreans to aid their fellow (Texas) Americans, once again at war with Mexico and the villainous Santa Anna. Two weeks after Houston's impassioned speech, the company named "Baltimore and Washington's Own" was brigaded with troops from the District of Columbia and mustered into service under the

## PATTERN #73: Strawberry Wreath III.

### Fourth page

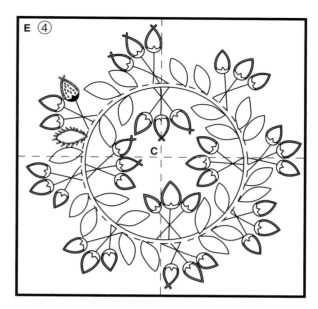

command of Lt. Colonel William H. Watson. Just four months later, Watson died gloriously, defending Monterrey. The Albums contain both written and emblematic references to the Mexican War, including specific memorials to Baltimore's ranking heroes, Colonel Watson and Major Ringgold.

The American flag that "Baltimore's Own" had brought along "from the patriotic women of Baltimore" flew victoriously from Monterrey's capitol. The Gray boys' verse could be interpreted to refer to a flag. Thus we have two possibilities—the women of Baltimore's American flag (returned to the City by the returning regiment) or the Texan's flag of the New Orleans Grays, a standard of courage eventually captured and sent back to Mexico City by Santa Anna. That trophy (pictured in *Stitched in Cloth, Carved in Stone*, a sequel to the *Baltimore Beauties and Beyond, Volume III*) remains in Mexico City to this day. We have ample evidence, a decade or so later in the 19th century, of ladies' aid societies supporting their cause in the Civil War. Might we, in these quilts, be seeing the tip of a fundraising effort by the Ladies of Baltimore? Would fundraising be needed for the flag sent by the Baltimore women? Or does the inscription to the Gray Boys refer to the more symbolic protection of the "token of Friendship" (this block, this quilt), which must be "guarded from insult" and "shielded from spoil"? Given the romantic phraseology and sensibilities of the day, either interpretation is possible and is pursued further in this book's sequel.

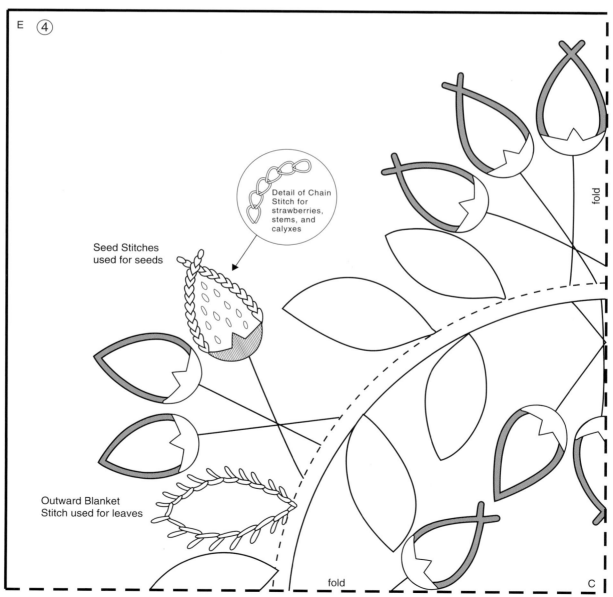

Detail of Chain Stitch for strawberries, stems, and calyxes

Seed Stitches used for seeds

Outward Blanket Stitch used for leaves

fold

## PATTERN #74: Dove and Lyre.

**Type: Baltimore-Style.** (From Quilt #2 in *Volume I*)

To make this block, refer to *Volume I*, Lessons 5 and 10, and to Appendix I in *Baltimore Album Quilts, Pattern Companion to Volume I.*

This classic block rings the themes we've come to love: doves, lyres, flowers, and wreaths. It has been included to give you yet one more of the ornate Victorian Album Blocks to stitch into rebirth in your Album.

**PATTERN #74: Dove and Lyre.**

**Second page**

**PATTERN #74: Dove and Lyre.**

**Third page**

**PATTERN #74: Dove and Lyre.**

**Fourth page**

## PATTERN #75: Album in a Rose Lyre Wreath.

**Type: Classic Baltimore.** (From Quilt #11 in *Volume II*)

To make this block, refer to Lessons 2 and 10 in *Volume I.*

Books recur repeatedly in Album blocks. "The book," the Bible, was used emblematically by the Odd Fellows to represent "Truth" in their motto "Friendship, Love, and Truth." (Friendship was symbolized by a shepherd's staff and tent, Love by the dove with olive branch.) Books in the old Album Quilts are diversely labeled: Bible, Hymns, Sacred Hymns, Al-

**PATTERN #75: Album in a Rose Lyre Wreath.**

**Second page**

bum, and Lady's Album. Entwined in roses, endearing, enduring friendship seems this block's theme. Yvonne Suutari has embroidered this reproduction exquisitely, using white machine-embroidery thread, single strand, to hand-embellish the roses in fine buttonhole stitch. You could ink the decoration and title on the Album, or you could simplify it and embroider it in chain stitch as Yvonne has done. She reverse appliquéd the book's binding.

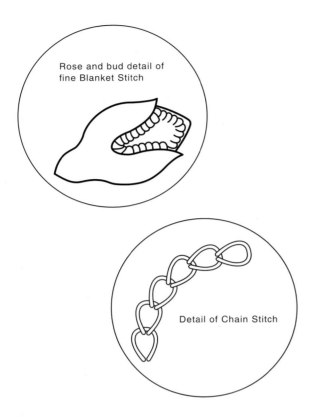

Rose and bud detail of fine Blanket Stitch

Detail of Chain Stitch

**DETAILS FROM PATTERN #75: Album in a Rose Lyre Wreath.**

**Third page**

Often in Album Quilts, the books look upside down. For an example, see The Album (Color Plate #24), reproduced by Letty Martin. In such renditions, the writing is right-side up, but the binding and the ribbon bookmarks (often red, yellow, and blue) look appropriate to a book reversed. While we can never be precisely certain what this iconography intends, it occurs with such frequency that I think it may depict the book (the Bible, the friendship Album, the sacred hymnal, the memory Album) opening heavenward for the sweetness of the good spirit to rise therefrom. Frequently, the book is not labeled, leaving us to wonder if the good spirit comes from friendship or from sacred script. But this imagery (like the flowers representing the sweet soul rising from an urn or vase) is one that the ladies of Baltimore were clearly fond of!

**PATTERN #76: Tree of Life.**

**Type: Baltimore-Style.** (Block F-5 from the Metropolitan Museum of Art's Album Quilt, Photo 26 in *Volume I*)

To make this block, refer to *Volume I,* Lessons 2 and 10.

The Tree of Life is an ancient symbol going far back to early civilizations. It seemed we couldn't finish our Album Quilt series without including a pattern for this classic Album block. A color version of this block is pictured in the East Bay Heritage Quilters' Album, Quilt #14 in *Volume II*.

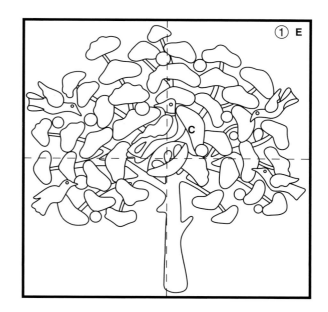

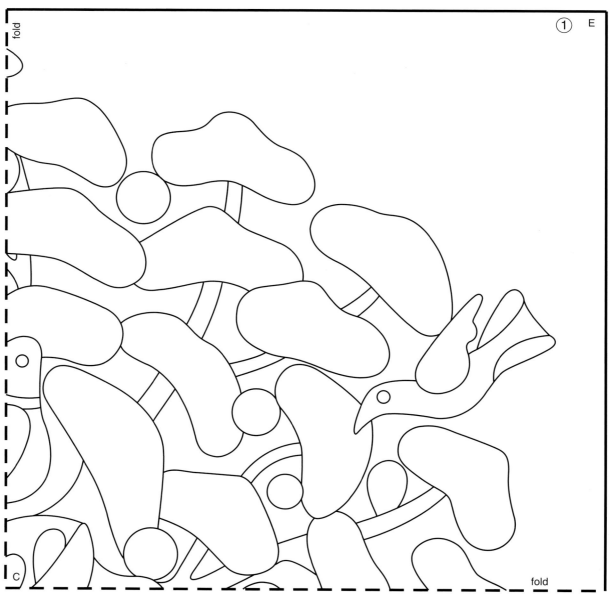

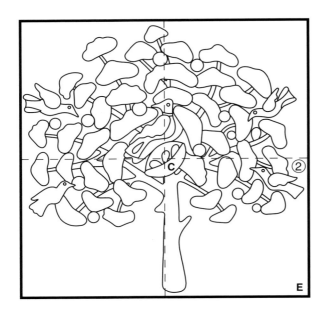

**PATTERN #76: Tree of Life.**

**Second page**

**PATTERN #76: Tree of Life.**

**Third page**

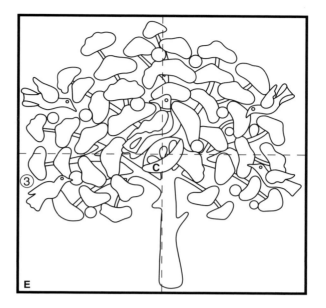

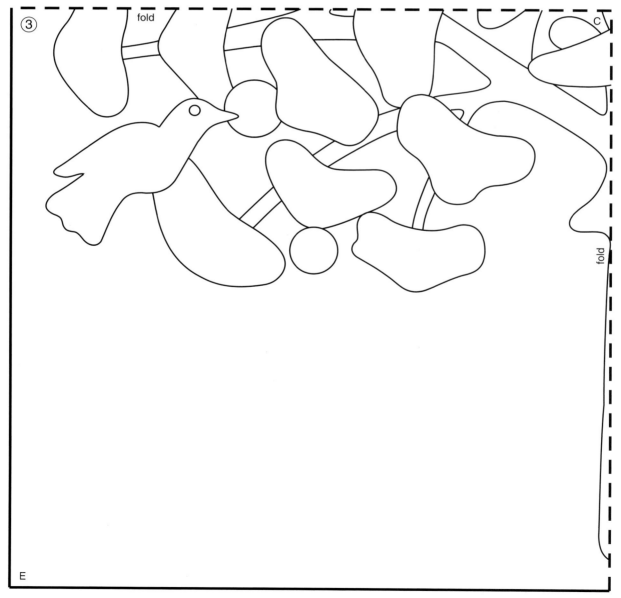

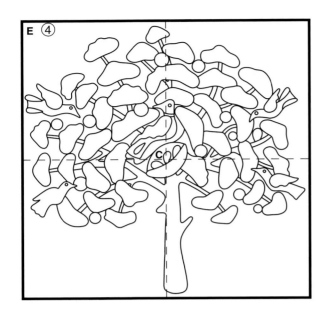

**PATTERN #76: Tree of Life.**

**Fourth page**

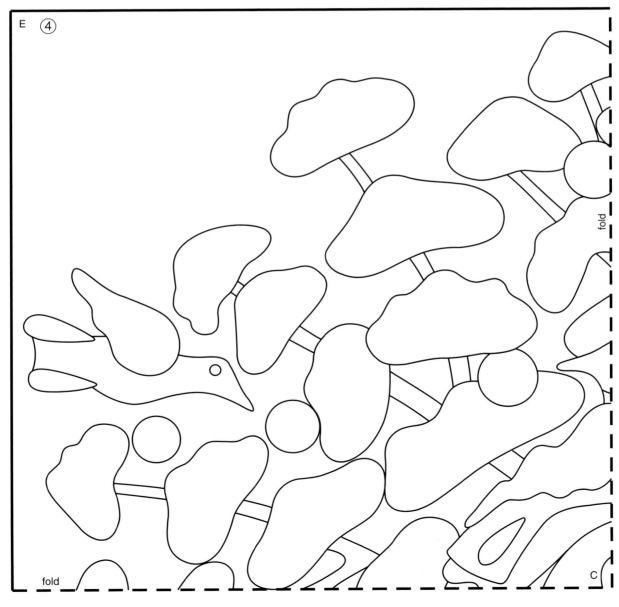

## PATTERN #77: Victorian Basket of Flowers III.

### Type: Baltimore-Style

To make this block, refer to *Volume I*, Lessons 5, 9, and 10. Also see Appendix I in *Baltimore Album Quilts, Pattern Companion to Volume I.*

Yet another extravagant, exquisite classic basket! The pattern has been faithfully drawn from Block B-3 in Quilt #2 in *Volume I*. See that photograph for a full-color model.

**PATTERN #77: Victorian Basket of Flowers III.**

**Second page**

**PATTERN #77: Victorian Basket of Flowers III.**

**Third page**

**PATTERN #77: Victorian Basket of Flowers III.**

**Fourth page**

**PATTERN #78: Basket of Full-Blown Roses.**

**Type: Classic Baltimore**

To make this block, refer to *Volume I,* Lessons 5, 9, and 10.

With delightful informality, this block's original appears to be a symmetrical arrangement that slipped in the sewing into a relaxed asymmetry. You can see that antique block in Quilt #3 in *Baltimore Album Quilts, Pattern Companion to Volume I.* Marian Johnson's reproduction echoes the wool embroidery of the original but takes the colors beyond Baltimore with her favorite dusty pinks.

The early Album scholar, Dr. William Rush Dunton, Jr., attributed the woolwork in the Baltimore-style Albums to a strong German

French knots

Straight Stitch wool embroidered leaf detail

fold

### PATTERN #78: Basket of Full-Blown Roses.

### Second page

influence (born of large German emigrations to Baltimore in mid-century). The wool stitchery is usually straight-stitching, sometimes in a scallop pattern, more often as close whipstitching or discrete straight stitches rhythmically spaced around a leaf or a bud. Sometimes looped embroidery stitches were also done in the wool thread. DMC's Medici® is a marvelous wool currently available for hand-embroidery. Annie Tuley, a machine needleartist, recommends a relatively new wool thread for embroidering such a block by machine. Called "Renaissance," this rich-looking wool is distributed by Sew Art International in Bountiful, Utah.

**PATTERN #78: Basket of Full-Blown Roses.**

**Third page**

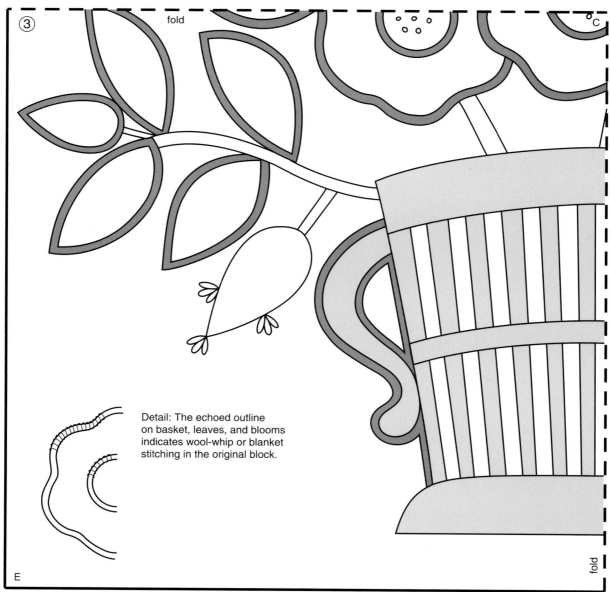

Detail: The echoed outline on basket, leaves, and blooms indicates wool-whip or blanket stitching in the original block.

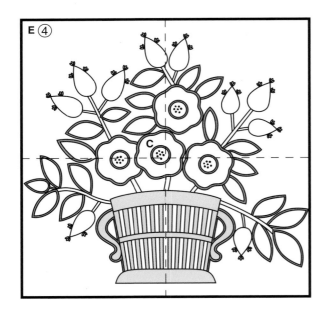

**PATTERN #78: Basket of Full-Blown Roses.**

**Fourth page**

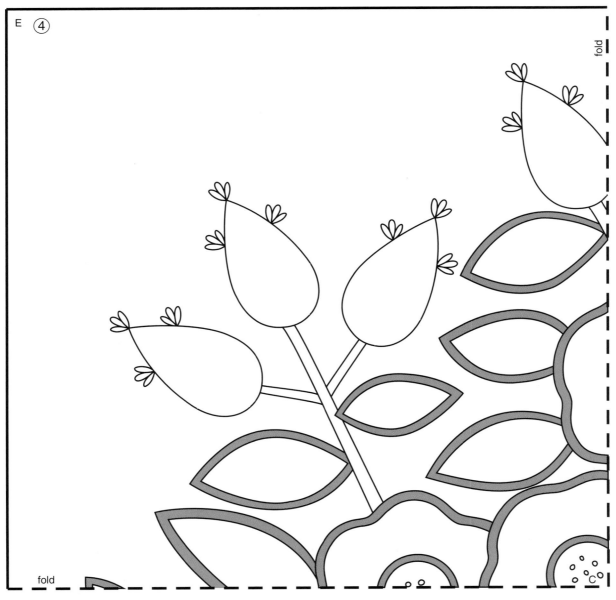

## PATTERN #79: Geranium Bird.

### Type: Baltimore-Style

To make this block, refer to *Volume I*, Lessons 2, 5, 9, and 10.

This pattern is by an antebellum needleartist whom I've dubbed "The Whimsical Botanist." Her hand seems distinctive in some or all of the blocks in Quilt #6 in *Dimensional Appliqué.* Marjo Hodges did this book's charming replica of this block. She made perfect tiny yellow circle centers in the flowers, chain-stitched their fine stems, and came up with a clever solution to the wee buds: She machine-seamed (using a tiny stitch) a 1" x 12" strip of

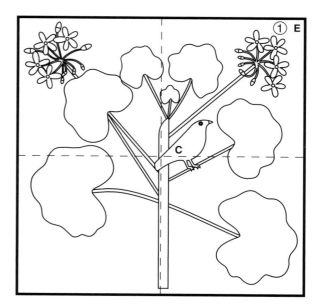

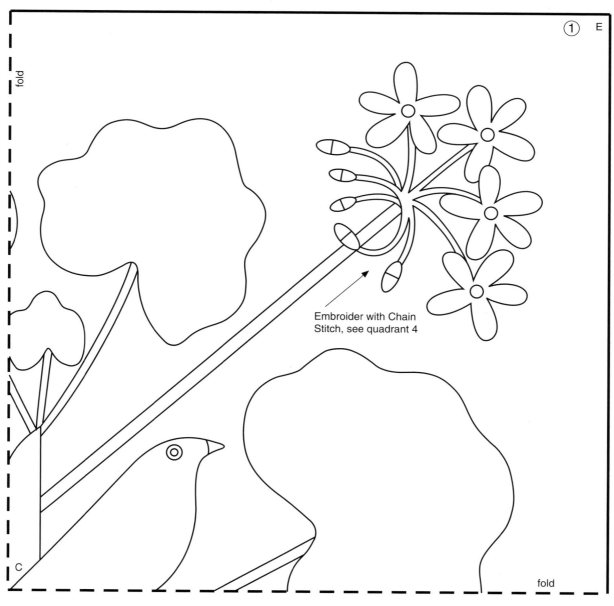

Embroider with Chain Stitch, see quadrant 4

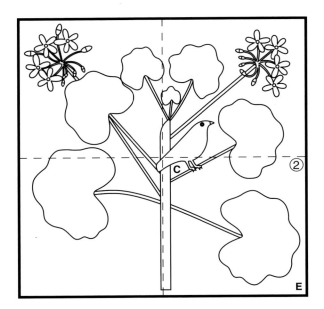

## PATTERN #79: Geranium Bird.

### Second page

red, right sides together with a same-size strip of green. Her seam was ⅛", trimmed back to ¹⁄₁₆" and pressed open after machining. Out of this red/green strip, she cut the buds, which were drawn with the appliqué seam allowance added on. From the collared look of the center stem-tip, to the straight-jutting leaf and flower stems, this block shows the quintessential geranium. No wonder this bird looks so content here! Another tree-perched bird in this

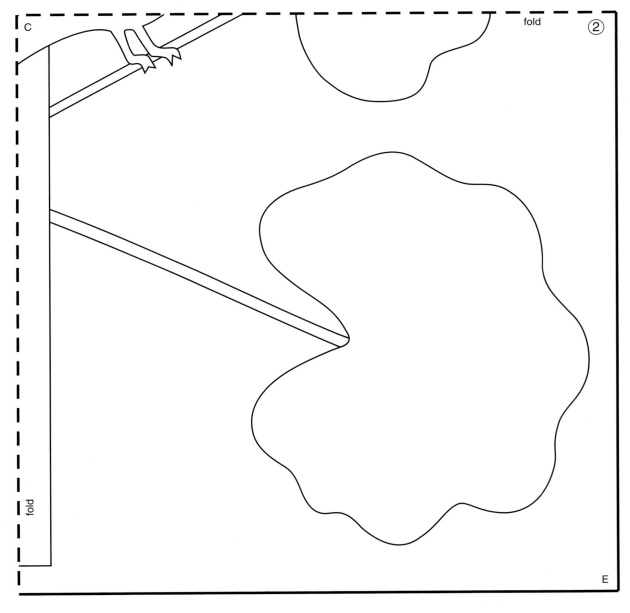

**PATTERN #79: Geranium Bird.**

**Third page**

same quilt has wee embroidered words, as if in song, coming from its beak. Unfortunately, I saw it hung at the Museum of American Art in Washington, D. C. It was protected there by an electronic "fence," which set off an alarm each time I craned upwards to try to read the words! But the idea is delightful: sweet messages sung to posterity by an appliquéd warbler.

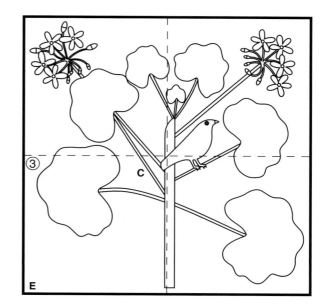

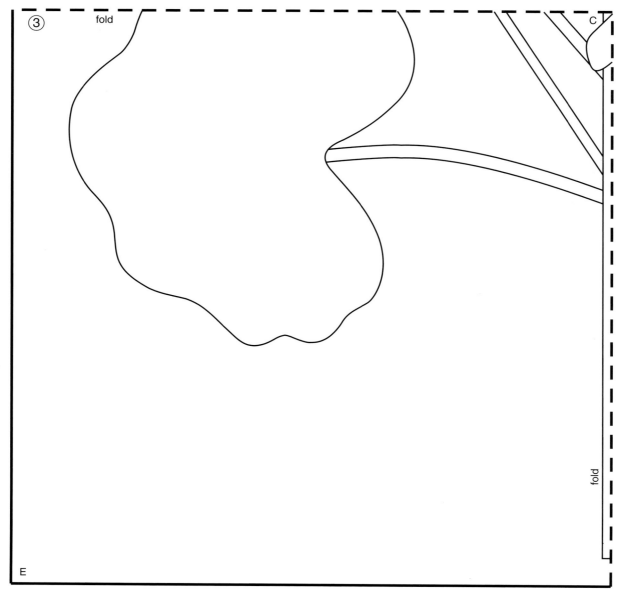

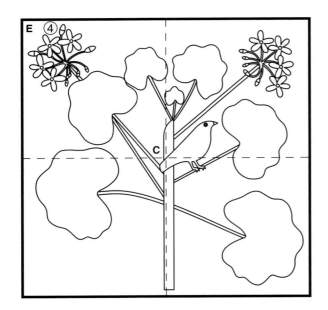

**PATTERN #79: Geranium Bird.**

**Fourth page**

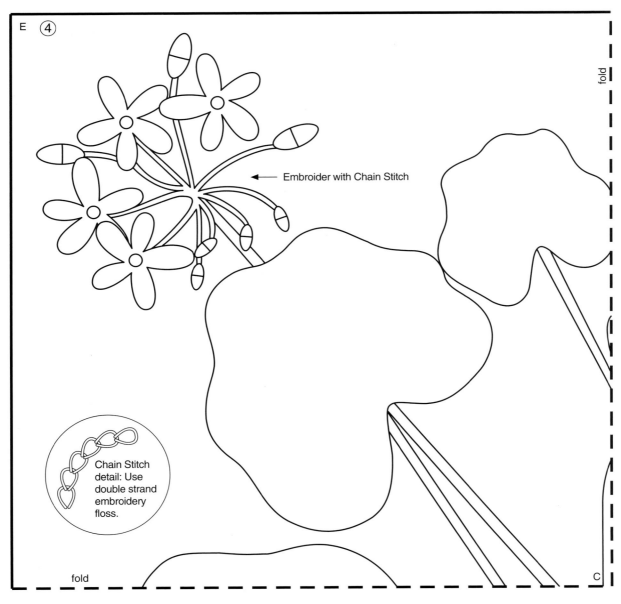

← Embroider with Chain Stitch

Chain Stitch detail: Use double strand embroidery floss.

**PATTERN #80: Half-Wreath of Blooms from Mrs. Mann's Quilt.**

**Type: Classic Baltimore**

To make this block, refer in *Volume I,* to Lessons 2, 5, 9, 10.

*Design a Baltimore Album Quilt!* discusses all the multiple forms that wreaths take in the classic Albums. This pattern might be a half wreath, or it might simply be a stem laden to the point of falling groundward with weight. It is a repeated, though not common, block in the Albums. In Mrs. Mann's quilt (Quilt #3 in *Baltimore Album Quilts, Pattern Companion to Volume I),* the use of two of these blocks is

**PATTERN #80: Half-Wreath of Blooms from Mrs. Mann's Quilt.**

**Second page**

effective. It would be interesting to see two of these blocks adjacent and mirroring one another, or four of them arranged as a repeat block center as in Quilts #7 and #8 in *Volume I*. Quilts like #6 in *Volume I*, which frame more complex center blocks with predominantly red-and-green ones, will always welcome this kind of simple classic Album block.

**PATTERN #80: Half-Wreath of Blooms from Mrs. Mann's Quilt.**

**Third page**

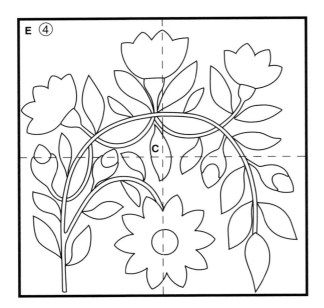

**PATTERN #80: Half-Wreath of Blooms from Mrs. Mann's Quilt.**

**Fourth page**

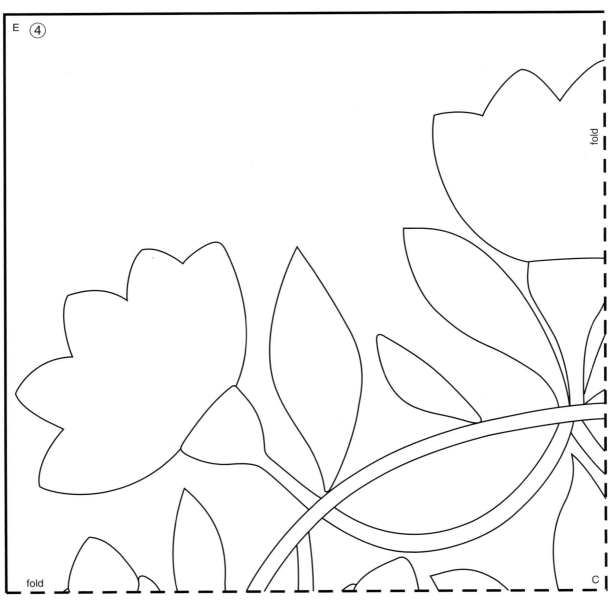

**PATTERN #81: Love Birds on a Rose Perch.**

**Type: Baltimore-Style**

To make this block, refer to *Volume I*, Lessons 5, 7, 9, or 10.

These roses are stuffed and quilted ones taught in *Dimensional Appliqué's* Lesson 7. Here, Barbara Hain stitched these roses in three pieces: First she appliquéd, stuffed, then quilted the tight inner petals of polished red cotton at the rose's top. Next she applied a sprigged yellow print center and appliquéd the large red lower rose petals. When the rose was fully stuffed, she closed the opening left in its base and quilted its petals.

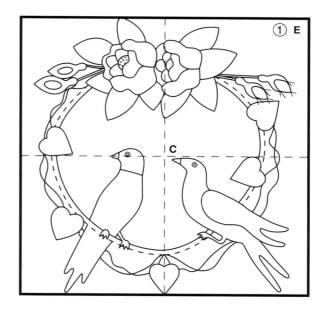

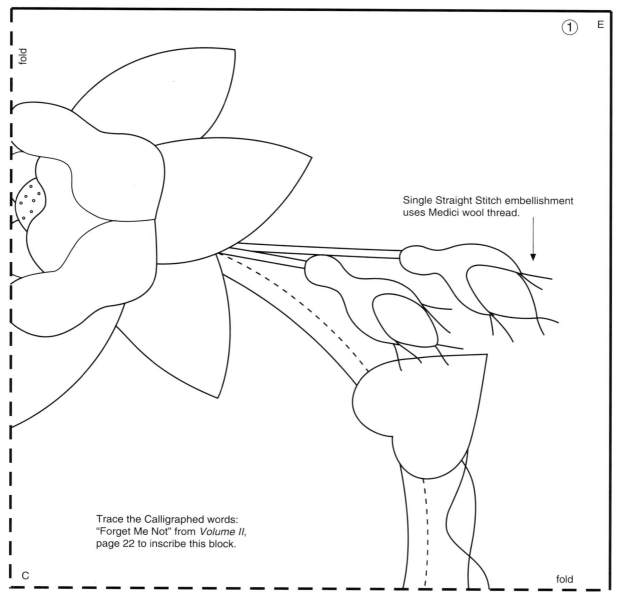

fold

Single Straight Stitch embellishment uses Medici wool thread.

Trace the Calligraphed words: "Forget Me Not" from *Volume II*, page 22 to inscribe this block.

C

fold

**PATTERN #81: Love Birds on a Rose Perch.**

**Second page**

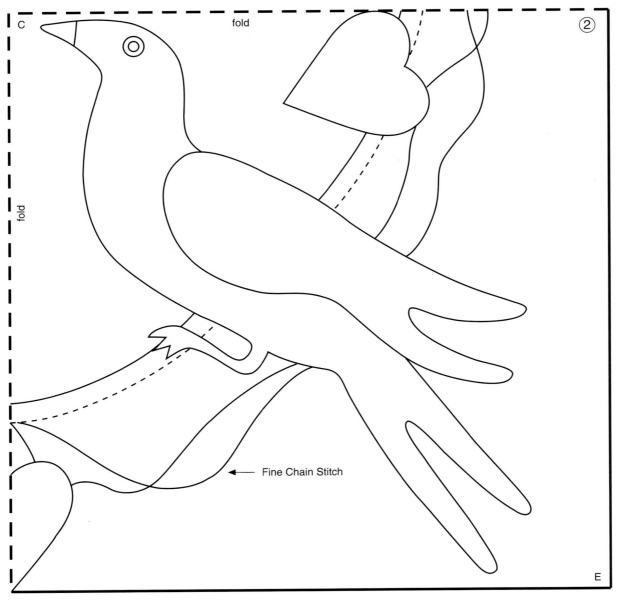

Fine Chain Stitch

## PATTERN #81: Love Birds on a Rose Perch.

### Third page

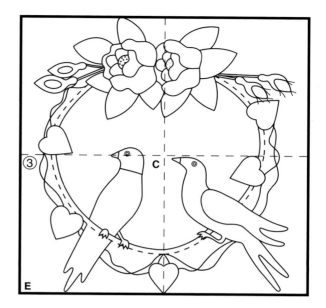

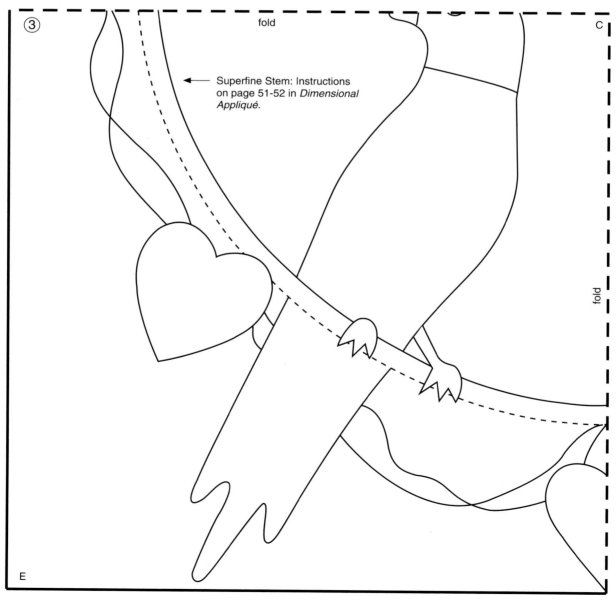

③

fold

Superfine Stem: Instructions
on page 51-52 in *Dimensional
Appliqué.*

C

fold

E

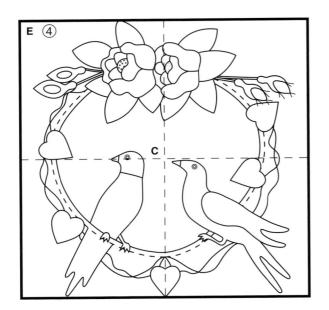

**PATTERN #81: Love Birds on a Rose Perch.**

**Fourth page**

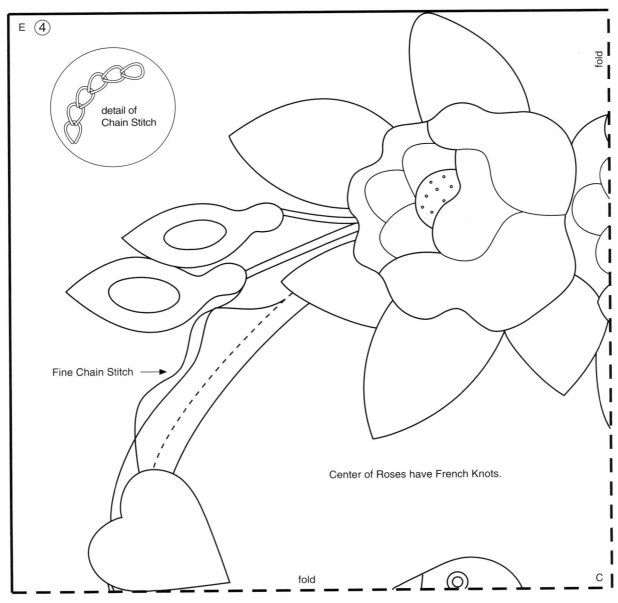

detail of
Chain Stitch

Fine Chain Stitch →

Center of Roses have French Knots.

fold

**PATTERN #82: Red Bird on a Passion Flower Branch.**

**Type: Baltimore-Style.** (From Quilt #6 in *Dimensional Appliqué)*

To make this block, refer to Lesson 7; in *Volume I*, Lessons 5, 9, and 10.

This seems to be another block pattern by "The Whimsical Botanist's" hand in "May You, My Child, in Virtue's Path Proceed," Quilt #6 in *Dimensional Appliqué*. The tropical Passion Flower comes in purple, red, or white with touches of blue and purple. It was named by the Spaniards (who first saw it in South America) because they thought it symbolized the story of the Crucifixion. Ever since I read Dr. Dunton's reference to

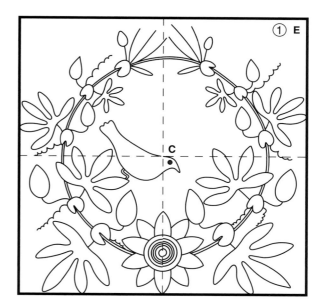

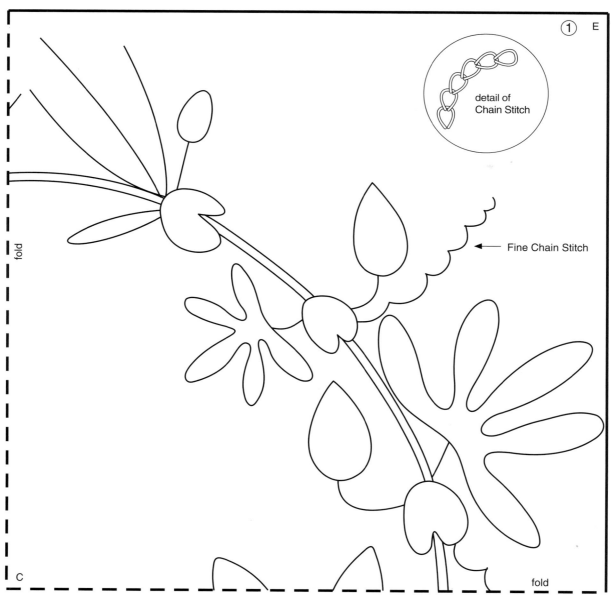

detail of Chain Stitch

◄── Fine Chain Stitch

**PATTERN #82: Red Bird on a Passion Flower Branch.**

**Second page**

Passion Flowers in *Old Quilts,* this flower has intrigued me. Brenda Green kindly brought me both a fresh Passion Flower blossom from her Florida garden and this quote ("to help with the symbolism") from *Palms and Flowers of Florida:* "The fringed corona represents the halo about Christ's head, or, the crown of thorns; the pistil is for the three nails; the five stamens are five wounds; the sepals and petals stand for ten of the disciples; the young seed pod is the vinegar-soaked sponge; the tendrils are the whips; the leaves (three- or five-lobed) represent the hands of Christ."

**PATTERN #82: Red Bird on a Passion Flower Branch.**

**Third page**

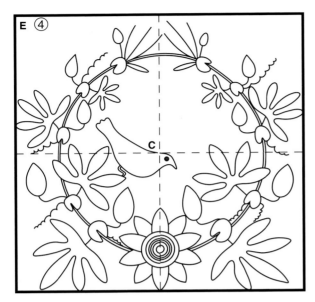

**PATTERN #82: Red Bird on a Passion Flower Branch.**

**Fourth page**

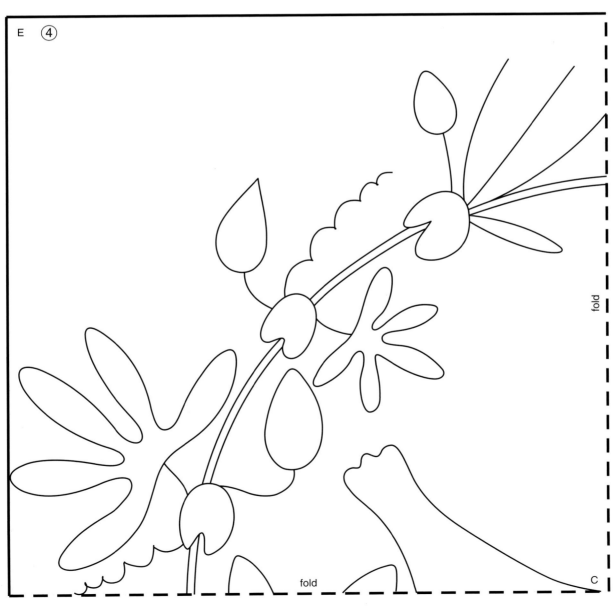

**PATTERN #83: Folk Art Bird.**

**Type: Baltimore-Style**

To make this block refer to *Volume I*, Lessons 5, 7, 9, or 10.

This graphic bird is in the style we often think of as Pennsylvania German. It is a strong, repeated style in the Baltimore Album Quilts and may indeed reflect the German influence therein. A peacock might have been included in the Album Quilts for emblematic reasons, for it is an ancient symbol of immortality. Then, too, its tail medallions are icons for the All-Seeing Eye of God. Since the All-Seeing Eye was a prime symbol of God's omniscience

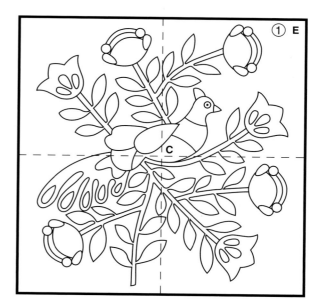

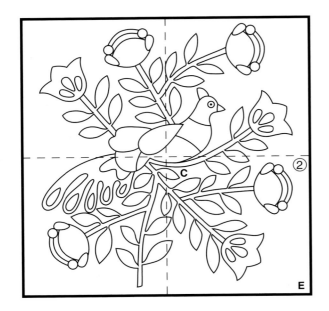

**PATTERN #83: Folk Art Bird.**

**Second page**

for both the Masons and the Odd Fellows, the peacock seems one more clear instance of intentional symbolism in the Baltimore-style Album Quilts.

**PATTERN #83: Folk Art Bird.**

**Third page**

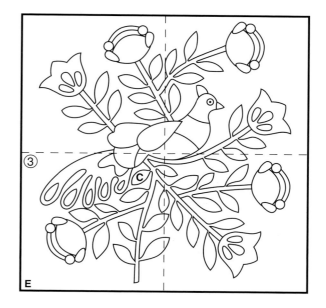

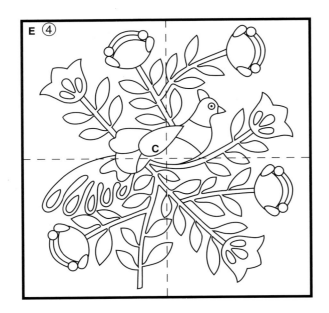

**PATTERN #83: Folk Art Bird.**

**Fourth page**

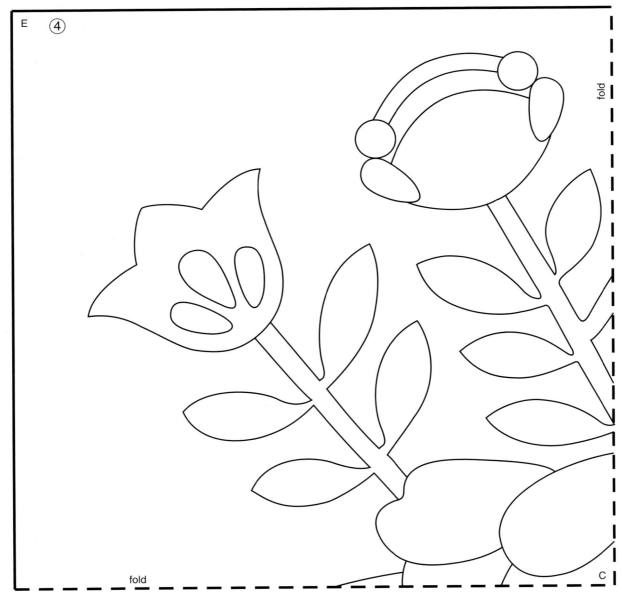

**PATTERN #84: Epergne of Fruit III.**

**Type: Classic Baltimore**

To make this block, refer to Lessons 1 and 2, and in *Volume I*, Lessons 5, 7, 9, or 10.

Technology and ideology may both beam from this elegant display of fruit. The Industrial Revolution swelled the ranks of the middle class and brought them new wealth. Decorative style on all fronts was diverse and in rapid transition. Though some of the changes might seem to us to be small details, for the middle-class homemaker, they were exciting opportunities for self-expression. In glassmaking for example, the 1830s ushered in the new technique of pressed glass. In

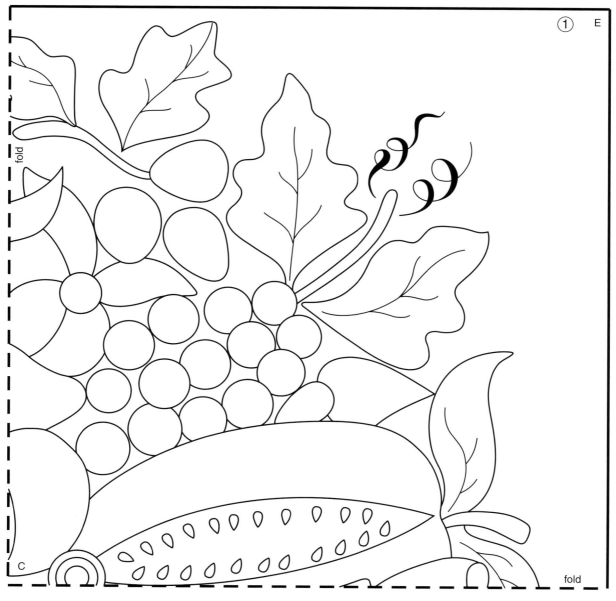

## PATTERN #84: Epergne of Fruit III.

### Second page

tableware, compotes, and epergnes, those neo-classical raised-glass dishes, which show off fruits as beautifully as a vase does flowers, made an *au courant* fashion statement. Often this glassware is stitched into the Albums in the cerulean or indigo blue we identify with Baltimore: Blue was a symbolic color, the color of truth and the soul.

A prime Odd Fellow symbol is the cornucopia overflowing with the bounty and the blessings of this earth. In the baskets and bowls of fruits, we probably see the same gratitude expressed. Perhaps this was a modi-

**PATTERN #84: Epergne of Fruit III.**

**Third page**

fiction dear to the Rebekahs. Or perhaps the symbolism was so apparent all would understand these variants. Clear delight seems to have been taken in depicting fruits and flowers with realistic touches (evidence of the beatitude of closely observing God's plan). Here in *Volume III*, we're focusing on touches of genius in fruit portrayal. With Kate Fowle's skillful fabric use, stenciling, and inking, this particular pattern sets us a stellar example to follow.

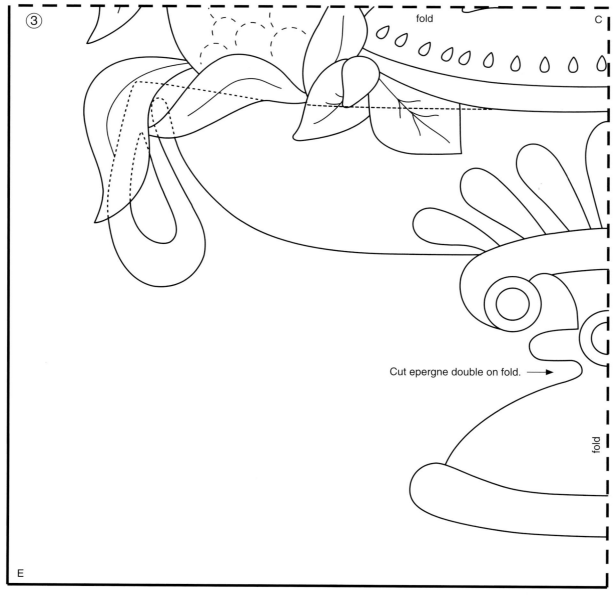

Cut epergne double on fold. →

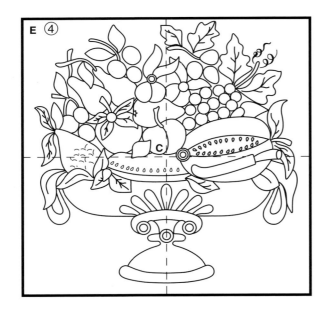

**PATTERN #84: Epergne of Fruit III.**

**Fourth page**

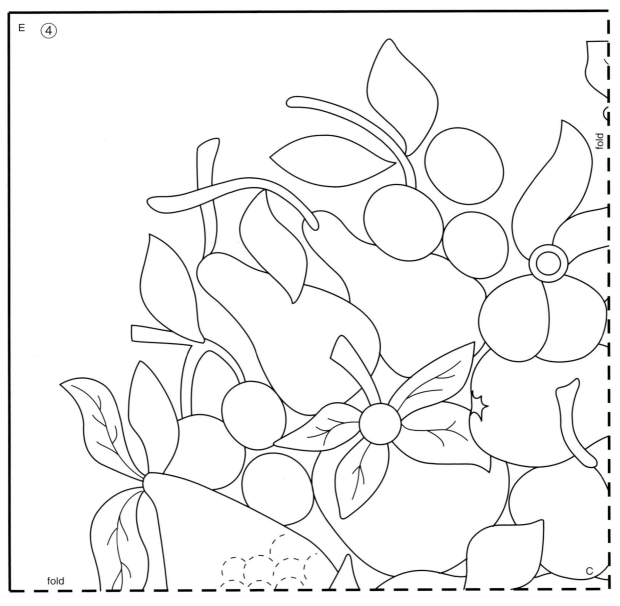

## PATTERN #85: Epergne of Fruit IV.

**Type: Classic Baltimore.** (From a Numsen family quilt shown in *Stitched in Cloth, Carved in Stone,* the sequel to *Volume III*)

To make this block, refer to Lessons 1 and 2, and in *Volume I,* Lessons 5, 7, 9, or 10.

Wendy Grande drafted this pattern from a picture of one of the Numsen Family Quilts. She was inspired to experiment with gauging, an old and little-known needlework technique, which involves a systematic shrinking of a shape from a larger to a smaller size by shirring its fabric. The technique (taught here in Lesson 1) sounded as though

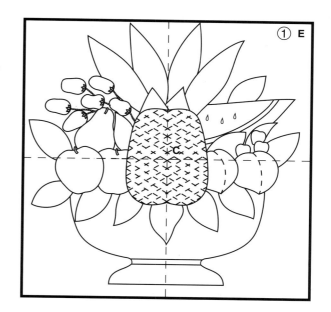

## PATTERN #85: Epergne of Fruit IV.

### Second page

it would make a wonderful pineapple. And it did! Wendy then went on to portray her local California olallaberries, again, with gauging. In the process she's made a perfectly wonderful block, which delights and inspires us with its graphic dynamism. It makes me want to slip into easier Album appliqués and so continue on, savoring the companionship of fellow Album-makers and sweet sentiments, well into the twilight of my life!

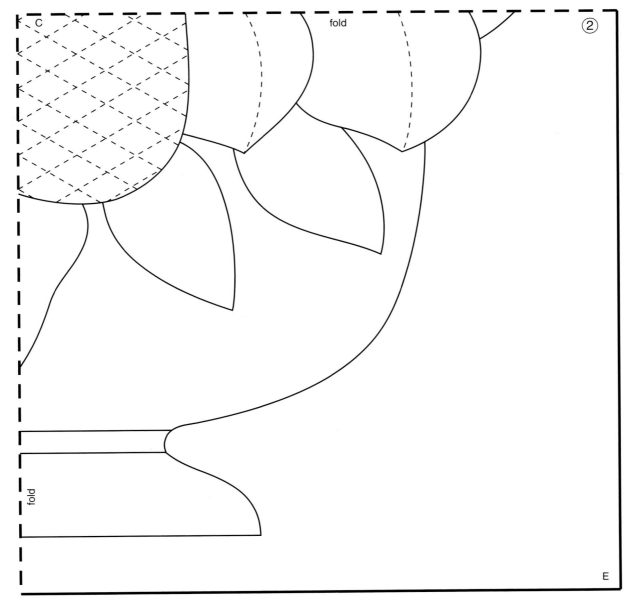

**PATTERN #85: Epergne of Fruit IV.**

**Third page**

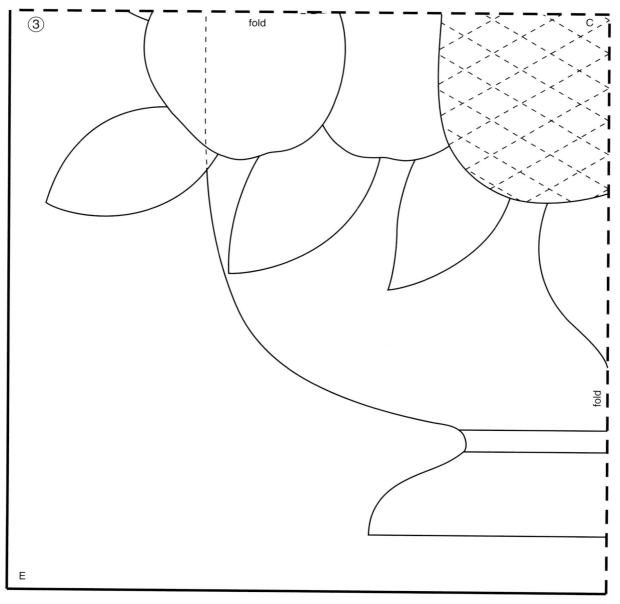

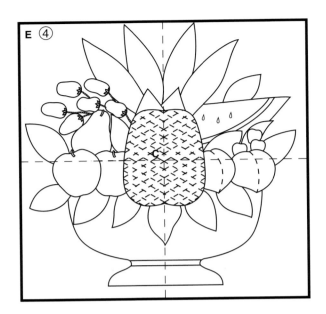

**PATTERN #85: Epergne of Fruit IV.**

**Fourth page**

E ④

*Note:* The berry stems are Outline or Stem stitch (see page 118). Lazy Daisy stitches (see page 25) cup the base of the berries.

fold

fold

C

# APPENDIX 1: CLASSES ————————————————

The following seven classes are for any teachers who care to teach them at shops or symposia, or for independent study, or for Baltimore Album sewing circles. These classes present either *Volume III* material or draw on the accumulated techniques of the *Baltimore Beauties* series. You have the author's and the publisher's permission to reproduce this Appendix class material. In addition, most classes require patterns, which each student can individually trace out of the *Baltimore Beauties* books beforehand and bring to class.

I. A HALF-DAY OR EVENING (THREE HOUR) CLASS THAT MAKES PARTICIPANTS EAGER TO GO ON AND TAKE YOUR BLOCK-A-MONTH PAPERCUT ALBUM CLASS.

*Baltimore Album Papercut Appliqué Made Easy! Intensive, Delightful Introduction to the Albums and to Their Techniques:*
    Learn whole-cloth cut-away appliqué (Elly's favorite), Freezer Paper on Top pattern transfer, and needleturn, while you begin a wonderful block from *Papercuts and Plenty, Volume III* of Elly Sienkiewicz's *Baltimore Beauties* series. Special attention to perfect points, curves, and corners. Leave class able to do the most versatile form of appliqué: needleturn with hidden stitches. (See the class model, a version of "Double Hearts," Block E-1 (Pattern #48 from *Volume III*) in Quilt #6, Classic Revival: Alex's Album. This class teaches the beginning Baltimore techniques of Lessons 1 and 2 in *Volume I*, teaches you how to inscribe a block in permanent ink, teaches you how to fold for a papercut design of your own, and gets you well started!
*Skill Level:* All.
*Materials Needed: Basic Sewing Kit:* #10-11 Sharps or Milliner's needles; small cut-to-the point paper and fabric scissors, thread to match appliqué, small straight pins, thimble, a Pigma "SDK"® .01 permanent pen in black for Album inscription, a dark fabric marking pencil (in case you want to draw around the freezer paper pattern and remove it), an iron. *Fabric:* Two 16" squares: one of background cloth; one of an interesting print (red or your color choice) for the appliqué. *Volume I* would be useful for its how-to drawings. *Note:* You need to bring Pattern #48 already traced in bold ink onto a 12½" square of freezer paper **but not cut out**. ("Getting Started" in *Volume I*, page 21, shows you how to fold the paper to take the pattern from the book.) Bring at least two more same-size squares of freezer paper to cut your own original version of our pattern.

————————————————  ————————————————

# CLASSES (continued) ——————————————————

II. A TEN-SESSION HALF-DAY OR EVENING (THREE HOUR) CLASS

*Come Join Our Baltimore-Style Papercut Album, Block A-Month Class!*

    *Volume I* of *Baltimore Beauties* devotes several Getting Started lessons to single-layer Album Quilt appliqué. *Volume III* takes these same simple, easy-to-learn appliqué techniques (needleturn with and without freezer paper) and guides you right on up to the realm of heirloom Papercut Album Quilts. Come create an heirloom! The first few patterns will be chosen by the teacher for specific techniques, then you can follow her lead or plan your own Album, even include your own designs! Your pace can be leisurely (one block a month) or intense. With this class, you'll become so confident in the fundamentals of exquisite hand appliqué that you'll probably want to continue next year in our "Album Sets, Borders, Quilting, and Binding Class"!

*Skill Level:* All.

*Materials Needed for First Class:* Bring a copy of *Papercuts and Plenty, Volume III of Baltimore Beauties and Beyond* for the patterns. Bring two 12½" squares of freezer paper to learn how to take your patterns from the book. *Basic Sewing Kit:* (#10-11 Sharps or Milliner's needles; small cut-to-the point paper and fabric scissors, thread to match appliqué, small straight pins, thimble, a Pigma "SDK"® .01 permanent pen in black, a dark fabric marking pencil (in case you want to draw around the freezer paper pattern and remove it), an iron. *Fabric:* Two 16" squares: one of background cloth; one of an interesting print (red or your color choice) for the appliqué. We'll talk about your color choices further in this first class. (*Volume I* and *Appliqué 12 Easy Ways!* are useful to bring for their how-to diagrams.)

———————————  ———————————

# CLASSES (continued)

III. A TWO-SESSION HALF-DAY OR EVENING (THREE HOUR) CLASS

*Fabulous Album Fruit Blocks!*
*—Tricks and Techniques:*
   Ready for one of Baltimore's fanciest blocks in layered, more realistic Victorian appliqué? Need a cornucopia of fruit in your Album collection? One made with exquisite ombré prints? Take the plunge by making this classic beauty and discover how easy its showy fruit is to appliqué! You'll learn all these skills for making complex blocks: pattern transfer and placement, layering, needleturn, "freezer paper inside" (and "on top"), hidden stitches, and inked embellishments. Learn how to use "print windows" to capture realism, stencil-shading fruit, "stem-well circles," and other Album-making "touches of genius." Our class model ("Cornucopia," Pattern #49, Color Plate 22, *Baltimore Album Quilts*) introduces the fundamental how-tos for the exquisite fruit blocks in *Papercuts and Plenty, Volume III* of Elly Sienkiewicz's *Baltimore Beauties and Beyond.*
*Skill Level:* Intermediate to Advanced.
*Materials Needed: Fabric:* 16" square background fabric; fat quarter of a print (suggest Elly Sienkiewicz's *Baltimore Beauties*® signature fabric "Ombré Leaves" in gold/rust from P&B Textiles) for the cornucopia. If you want to make it in stripes, bring scraps and begin at the cornucopia's bottom. Bring small scraps for fruit, greenery, and bird. Study fabric use in Color Plate 22. *Optional special fabrics:* tie-dyes, ombré prints, light to medium monochromatic prints for stencil-shading. Bring half yard of freezer paper, glue stick, sharp pencil for marking background, small sharp paper and fabric scissors, #11 Sharps or Milliner's needles, small straight pins, black or brown Pigma® pen .01 pen, enough ½" and ¾" "Office Dots" for the grapes and plums, an appropriate print or a couple of self-stick notebook reinforcers for inking stem-well circles (if you have them). Iron, extension cord, and cardboard notepad back as ironing board. Bring Artists' Paintstiks® (oil paint sticks from art supply store), if you have them. *Note:* Please bring Pattern #22 from *Baltimore Album Quilts* already traced in bold ink onto the four quadrants of a 12½" square of freezer paper **(but not cut out).** You can short-cut the process by photocopying the pattern and pasting its four quarters onto a square of freezer paper.

# CLASSES (continued)

IV. A TWO HALF-DAY OR TWO EVENING (THREE HOURS) SAMPLER CLASS THAT MAKES PARTICIPANTS EAGER TO GO ON TO YOUR EIGHT WEEK "BEGIN A BALTIMORE" CLASS. (Shops can provide an optional kit for busy ladies!)

*Quick-Start Baltimore Album:*
*The Folded Rosebud Wreath!*
    A Ribbon Rose replaces the bow, the inscription becomes "[name of your town and state]," in this spectacular "Introduction to Baltimore Appliqué" memento Album block. See the prototype wreath in Color Plate 21 in Elly's *Dimensional Appliqué.* Leave with a stitched souvenir of a happy afternoon [evening], having learned so much, so easily! Learn the basic techniques needed for Baltimore: Cut-away Appliqué by hand (perfect points, curves, corners, invisible stitches), layered appliqué, folded rosebuds, "Freezer Paper Inside" for the calyxes, and a rolled ribbon rose center. Make this an exquisite Album Quilt block. Or frame it. Even make it into a pillow!
*Skill Level:* All (Beginners welcome!)
*Materials Needed:* #11 Sharps, #10 Milliner's needles, "invisible" nylon thread for rose, matched green sewing thread, small, to-the-point paper and fabric scissors, pins, permanent black Pigma® .01 pen, masking tape. *Fabric:* Two 16" squares: one of off-white Album background cloth; the second of medium—large green "leaf" print with the following preparation done at home: "The Maine Wreath" (Pattern #3 in *Dimensional Appliqué)* cut out of freezer paper and tightly ironed, centered—shiny side down—to the right side of the green cloth. Cut nothing further. Bring 1½"-wide Shaded Wire-Edged Ribbon (3½" = rosebud, 1 yard = rose). Bring one yard each of three colors, which go well together: 3 yards total.

V. A THREE-HOUR CLASS THAT MAKES PARTICIPANTS WANT TO GO ON TO YOUR BLOCK-A-MONTH CLASS. (Optional kit for busy ladies!)

*Sample a Block-a-Month Baltimore*
*Bride Basket-Album!*
    Super-simple ribbon-woven baskets fill Quilt #4 in *Dimensional Appliqué.* Learn basket-making basics (even braided brims) and find how very easy they can be. We'll make a lush ribbon basket on Album block background—or, if you prefer, on a color for a "throw-pillow" background. Then we'll teach you a leaf and one quick ribbon rose, so you can fill your basket even if you decide not to make a whole Baltimore Basket-Album!
*Skill Level:* All (Beginners welcome!)
*Format:* Hands-on: Make an exquisite Album Quilt block. Or frame it! Make it into a pillow!
*Materials Needed:* #11 Sharps, #10 Milliner's needles, "invisible" nylon thread for rose, matched green sewing thread, small, cut-to-the-point paper and fabric scissors, pins, glue stick, masking tape. *Fabric:* 16" squares of off-white Album background cloth (or your choice cloth) with the following preparation done at home: With a bold pen, trace the outline (only) of Pattern #33 from *Dimensional Appliqué* off onto folded freezer paper. Cut the pattern out, double on the fold. Next, cut the pattern ⅛" smaller around its cut edges. Place this pattern—shiny-side down and lightly ironed—1" below the center of the right side of the background cloth. Draw around this shape and remove the pattern. Bring a tracing or a photocopy of the pattern, an 8" square cardboard to pin the basket ribbon into; Double-faced satin ribbon (dark green looks good; check ribbon for colorfastness). For Pattern #33, bring four yards of ¼"-wide ribbon, 1½ yards of ⅓"-wide (or closest ribbon sizes to these); For a rose: bring one yard of 1 ½"-wide shaded Wire-Edged Ribbon. Cut a freezer paper leaf "B" out from Pattern #13 in *Dimensional Appliqué.* Pin the leaf, shiny-side up, to the wrong side of a scrap of green and bring to class.

# CLASSES (continued) ———————————————

### VI. A FOUR HALF-DAY OR EVENING (THREE HOUR) CLASS

*A Della Robbia Wreath*
*(or Your Choice) Center Medallion!*

    This delightful class will net you a glorious center medallion for your Baltimore-Style Album Block Quilt or for a medallion-centered "Bordered Baltimore." Choose one of Elly Sienkiewicz's Baltimore Medallion Patterns from *Spoken Without a Word, Dimensional Appliqué* or *Appliqué 12 Borders and Medallions!* to work on in this class. Or, create your own stunning fruit or flower center medallion wreath based on the directions for Pattern #34 on pullout in *Dimensional Appliqué.* (This simply entails stitching a 10" radius stem-circle around the center of a 30" square of background cloth. You'll then bring it into fruit (for a Della Robbia Wreath) or bloom with patterned elements (taken from throughout the *Baltimore Beauties* series) and arranged to your own taste. Not sure which medallion to do? Come to the first class and we'll discuss them all and begin a wreath medallion. Consider this encouraging fact: Medallion-size appliqué is so easy compared to the smaller scale appliqué required for Album blocks!
*Skill Level:* Intermediate to Advanced
*Materials Needed:* Bring the book whose medallion pattern you wish to do. Bring freezer paper, glue stick, a pencil, paper scissors, an envelope. We'll discuss how to approach the appliqué and will cut the patterns in the first class. Bring two 30" squares of background cloth: one blank (on which to make a patterned medallion), one prepared with a 10" radius circle drawn around its center (on which to design your own medallion wreath). Cover this drawn circle with a "Superfine Stem" (page 51, *Dimensional Appliqué*). Begin with a 1⅛"-wide bias-cut green strip, folded in half, right-sides out, raw edges on the drawn line, the fold facing the block's center. Machine the initial seam, then press the fold to the outside of the circle and pin for class.

### VII. A HALF-DAY OR EVENING (THREE HOUR) CLASS

*Make an Album Block Carrying Case!*

    Need an "Album," a protective case to hold and display your Album blocks while you work on them? This elegant hard-backed Album Block Case designed by Jo Anne Cardone Maddalena is the perfect carrier/storage place for your Album blocks as you make them. Remember, there is great pleasure, every stitch of the way to an Album Quilt, and finishing it can take a while. This case is just what you need while you enjoy the process. Come join us in this light, easy class filled with like-minded Album-makers!
*Skill Level:* All.
*Format:* Hands-on with a sewing machine
*Materials Needed:* Bring the cutting/assembly instructions and materials as listed in Appendix II, *Papercuts and Plenty, Volume III of Baltimore Beauties and Beyond, Studies in Classic Album Quilt Appliqué,* by Elly Sienkiewicz.

————————————————  ————————————————

# APPENDIX 2: ALBUM BLOCK CASE

## ALBUM BLOCK CASE
Design and Instructions by Jo Anne Maddalena

### Materials:
- 40" x 30" Illustration board, foam core, particle board, or any other sturdy cardboard. (Cut this into two precise 18" squares and one 6½" x 18" rectangle.)
- X-Acto® knife to cut cardboard. If you use particle board or foam core, you can often have it cut to size where you purchase it.
- 1⅓ yards of fabric A (Outside of case)
- 1⅓ yards of fabric B (Lining of case)
- Sewing machine
- Thread to match fabrics

### Preparing the Fabric:
*For case:* Cut fabrics A (Outside) and B (Lining), one long rectangle from each: 48" x 18½"

*For side flaps:* Again cut fabrics A and B, two rectangles from each: 18½" x 6½"

*For ties:* Cut fabric A or B into two strips: 1¼" x 26"

*For handle:* Cut fabric A into one strip: 1¾" x 9"

### Piece the Side Flaps:
Place the two sets of 18½" x 6½" rectangles right sides together (one fabric A and one fabric B per set). Stitch, using a ¼" seam allowance, around two short sides and one long side. Clip corners and turn. Press.

### Sew the Ties:
Fold the two 1¼" x 26" strips lengthwise, right sides together, and stitch ⅜" from fold. Insert a safety pin in fold side ½" from one end. Push safety pin through casing to turn right side out. Press and cut each piece in half (resulting in four 13" ties).

### Make the Handle:
Fold the 1¾" x 9" strip right sides together and stitch ⅝" from fold. Turn as for ties. If a heavy feel is desired, insert a piece of batting inside. Top-stitch approximately ⅛" from each long side. Trim off end to measure 8½".

### Prepare the Outside:
Refer to Figure A-2 (following page) as you pin and stitch the following items onto the right side of the long rectangle of outside Fabric A:

1. *Side Flaps:* Pin flaps (outside Fabric A), raw edges together, to the outside Fabric A of the Album Case cover; pinning on each long side, 7¾" from the top flap. Baste the flaps in place. You'll machine stitch them when the outside of the case is completely prepared and the flaps and ties are "sandwiched" between the outside and the lining.

2. *Handle:* Turn under ½" on each end of the handle. Then pin this handle in the place (7⅛" down from the top and 6" in from each end) shown on Figure A-2. Stitch each end securely along the fold and again, ½" in from the first row of stitches.

3. *The Ties:* Baste two ties along top flap edge (6" in from each side so that they are centered on the case). Fold ½" under on the remaining two ties and pin 11½" from the front edge end and 6" from the side. Be sure that the ends of these are facing away from the body of the case, as in Figure A-2. Stitch by sewing a ¼" x ½" rectangle over the folded end.

### Finishing the Case:
Place the prepared outside right sides together with the lining. Pin the two long sides and the top (where the ties are). Be careful that the ties and flaps are tucked inside. Stitch using a ¼" seam allowance. Trim corners. Turn and press. Edge stitch close to the fold along the entire outside except the tube opening—this prevents shifting cardboard when finished.

Insert the 6½" x 18" piece of illustration board and stitch Line A in Figure A-2 along the edge of the board (a zipper foot works well here). Next, stitch Line B ⅞" beyond Line A; this forms the top flap and top.

Insert an 18" square of illustration board and stitch along edge (Line C) and again ⅞" beyond this along Line D; this forms the back and bottom.

Insert the last 18" square of illustration board. Turn inside remaining seam allowance (trim if necessary) and stitch closed.

Close the case and tie it shut. Trim ties to desired length. Tie a knot at the end of each. Enjoy!

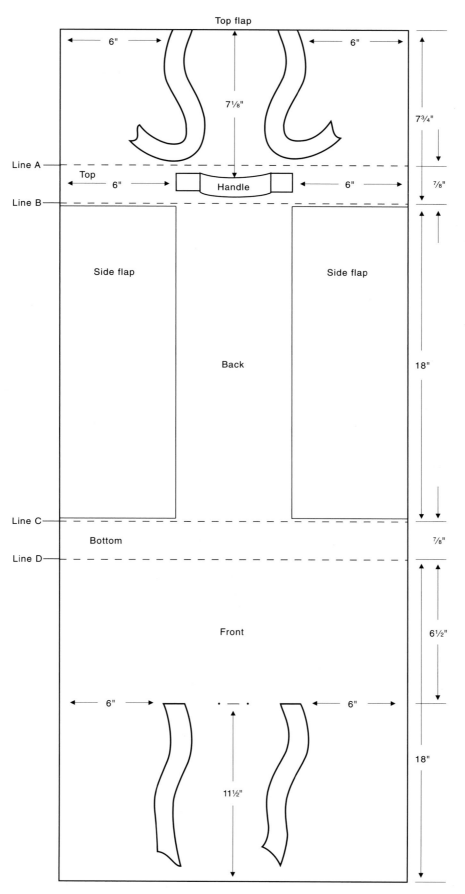

FIGURE A-2 Album Block Case designed by Jo Anne Maddalena. Diagram by Peter Maddalena.

# AUTHOR'S AFTERWORD

Making our Album blocks as well as reading and writing these Album books, has been a communion among friends. To think so frequently of those who made this style of quilt a century and a half ago, cannot but spiritually tie us to them. This closeness seems comforting to all who experience it. It is as though we gain a certain strength and wisdom from knowing not only the spirit in which women before us have stitched, but in understanding that throughout all, they persevered. Moreover they prevailed, having left behind them quilts with a message of lasting beauty—a beauty that sustains us still. We could only have been known to their imaginations, just as the thought comes, as we stitch, that some future soul will gain in pleasure and understanding from these quilted threads we leave behind. The very sense of one's life being interwoven with those who have come before, and with those who will come after, is an optimistic perspective—is satisfying, provides some warmth and sense of time and place in this vast universe that is our home. By making quilts we, too, bear witness to our faith in the future; we affirm that who we are, what we do, matters. It is as though we try, through stitched cloth, to convey our love not only for someone known to us, but for those yet to come. Our quilts, our soundless voices, intend and promise comfort.

Album makers of the late-20th century have come to feel a fellowship with each other, "as with those who journey together." That phrase has threaded through my life, words from a "Fireside Prayer" written by my clergyman grandfather, dead long before my father became a man. But his small framed statement hung soberly on the wall of the house where I grew up, and my child's imagination played with the image of people journeying together. At times I thought of pilgrims, at times of pioneers in covered wagons. Later, as a young school teacher, we spoke of "Spaceship Earth" to convey the interdependence of the world's inhabitants, all on a voyage together. But journeying in these infinite reaches of space, we need wellsprings of human warmth. Family is a good place to start; then comes community. For it seems clearly to be community—community of a most heartwarming sort—that we Album quilters have found with each other. So until we meet again in this book's sequel, I'd like to share those words from my grandfather with you. Perhaps your imaginations, too, will take wing as you stitch your Album squares—paeans to the past, the present, and the future. Thank you for joining me on what has become an odyssey. Persevere, and cherish moments spent on your Album making for "happiness is in the journey!"

---

### *A Fireside Prayer*

*Almighty God, who hath set the solitary in families, and loveth the dwellings of Jacob, we commit to Thy care our fireside. May our home be to us a holy of holies, a refuge from cares, a haven from storms, a fountain of joys, a shrine of peace. May the joy and sorrow of each of us be the joy and sorrow of all of us, as is the case with those who journey together. May love be the foundation beneath us, the walls around us, the roof over our heads, the bread by which we live. To each other may we give loyalty and confidence, to our friends hospitality and good cheer, to strangers welcome and refreshment. And may all be given gladly as unto Thee who art disguised in the sons of men, and wilt Thou give us Thy blessing of peace. This, the consecration of our fireside, we make for all the days of joy and sorrow, health and sickness, prosperity and adversity, which we shall share together. And for Thy name's sake. Amen.*

—Rollo Albert Hamilton

# INDEX

*to the* Baltimore Beauties
*Series Patterns, Quiltmakers,
and Techniques*

Key to books listed in the Index. Book abbreviations are followed by the page number. Annotated listings for books in the series may be found on page 205.

**Key to type of pattern:**

B = "Beyond" Baltimore, a quilt or block pattern beyond Baltimore in time or space
C = Classic Baltimore, a quilt or block pattern taken from a Baltimore Album quilt of the 19th century
P = Papercut or "Snowflake" pattern
S = Baltimore-Style pattern, a quilt or block pattern that looks like a mid-19th century quilt but has uncertain provenance
T = Traditional Appliqué pattern (not Baltimore-Style), whether antique or contemporary

**THE PATTERNS**

## THE QUILTMAKERS

## THE TECHNIQUES

# ABOUT THE AUTHOR

Eleanor Hamilton Sienkiewicz is a quiltmaker, teacher, and author whose interests in art, history, and religion are well met in the mid-19th-century Baltimore Album Quilts. With degrees from Wellesley College and the University of Pennsylvania, Elly has for a decade and a half, now, written about the Album Quilts and appliqué. With a connoisseur's enthusiasm, she probes the artistic, technical, historic, and philosophical depths of the antebellum Albums. No less intriguing to her is the question of what motivates the phenomenal Album work being done by contemporary quiltmakers. Mrs. Sienkiewicz's *Baltimore Album Revival!—Historic Quilts in the Making* suggests some possible answers.

The author's perception of Maryland's Album quilts is informed by perseverent historical research and a kindred quiltmaking passion. Her *Baltimore Beauties* series combines faithfully reproduced antique patterns with artistic "beyond Baltimore" interpretations. With clarity and inspiration, her ten books on Albums and appliqué twine how-to instruction together with history and insight into the very souls of the quiltmakers themselves. She is widely respected for her knowledge of the Baltimore Album Quilts in particular, and has increasingly been cited as the ranking authority on this classic quilt genre. Before she became so deeply involved with researching and writing on Album Quilts, Elly's own fabric art had been shown at major quilt shows around the country and at Glen Echo, The National Art Park; The Textile Museum; Decatur House; The Decorators' Showcase; and the Art Barn in Rock Creek National Park—all in the vicinity of Washington, D. C., where she lives with her husband and three children.

Consumed by the ongoing question of our current fascination with the Album style, Elly is a delightful teacher and an inspiring lecturer. Attesting to this fact, she has taught and lectured from the nearby Smithsonian Institution to as far away as Europe, New Zealand, South Africa, and Japan. Articles by and about Elly are widely published in such places as *The American Quilter*, *Quilter's Newsletter Magazine*, *Traditional Quilter*, *Traditional Quiltmaking*, *The Magazine Antiques*, *Folk Art Magazine*, *Victoria*, and *Threads*. A long-time resident of Washington, D. C., and Turtle Hill, Little Round Bay on-the-Severn, Maryland, Elly is well-situated to pursue the study of these antique Maryland quilts she loves so well.

## BOOKS BY ELLY SIENKIEWICZ

With the exception of her first, self-published book, the author's following books are available from C&T Publishing, P.O. Box 1456, Lafayette, California, 94549. 1-800-284-1114

*Spoken Without A Word —A Lexicon of Selected Symbols, With 24 Patterns from Classic Baltimore Album Quilts* (1983).

This was the first book to faithfully reproduce patterns from classic Baltimore Album Quilts and to point out the intentional symbolism within these quilts' design motifs. (Available from the author: 5540 30th Street, NW, Washington, DC 20015. Send $24.00 U.S. domestic postpaid, check made out to the author.)

*Baltimore Beauties and Beyond, Studies in Classic Album Quilt Appliqué, Volume I* (1989).

Twelve lessons take the beginner from the simplest Baltimore Album Quilt blocks to the most complex. A wealth of appliqué techniques is presented, and 24 Album block patterns are given. Already itself a classic, this book introduces you to Baltimore-style Album making.

*Baltimore Album Quilts, Historic Notes and Antique Patterns, A Pattern Companion to Baltimore Beauties and Beyond, Volume I* (1990).

A magnificent 56 patterns (all correlated to *Volume I's* lessons) offers the framework for sharing Baltimore's fascinating historical saga and closeup pictures of antique blocks and Albums.

*Baltimore Beauties and Beyond, Studies in Classic Album Quilt Appliqué, Volume II* (1991).

This volume pictures more than 50 antebellum Albums and offers 20 block and 13 border patterns. It teaches the design and making of Picture Blocks and instructs on how to write on your quilts in permanent ink, including the transfer of engraved motifs by ironed-on photocopies.

*Appliqué 12 Easy Ways! Charming Quilts, Giftable Projects, and Timeless Techniques* (1991).

A very basic how-to-appliqué book illustrated with wonderful clarity. Complete patterns include 29 beautiful projects from gifts to graphic museum replica quilts. Their common thread? All have immediate eye-appeal and are so easy to make! Written for the novice, this book has proven equally popular among experienced appliquérs wishing to learn Elly's "latest pointers" on appliqué.

*Design a Baltimore Album Quilt, A Design Companion to Volume II of Baltimore Beauties and Beyond, Studies in Classic Album Quilt Appliqué* (1992).

How do you set your diverse Album blocks into a magnificent quilt? What border suits them best? Elly's ingenious book provides 18 easy lessons and miniaturized blocks and borders for a unique "cut and paste" Album Quilt design system. Then there are instructions for how to make several antique bindings and all the patterns (including the border) for reproducing a lovely 25-block antique Baltimore Album Quilt.

*Dimensional Appliqué—A Pattern Companion to Volume II of Baltimore Beauties and Beyond, Studies in Classic Album Quilt Appliqué* (1993).

A best-seller! Simple, innovative methods for dimensional flowers and unique appliqué basketry. All are taught through step-by-step teach-yourself lessons, dozens of block patterns, and five border patterns. Whether for stylish clothing accessories or for an heirloom quilt, with this book, exquisite flowers bloom at your fingertips!

*Baltimore Album Revival! Historic Quilts in the Making—A Catalog to C&T Publishing's Baltimore Album Revival Quilt Show and Contest* (1994).

This catalog documents an historic 1994 Revivalist Album Quilt exhibition and contains an essay, as insightful as it is entertaining, analyzing why Baltimore-style Album Quilts have become so popular, once again.

*Appliqué 12 Borders and Medallions! Patterns from Easy to Heirloom—A Pattern Companion to Volume III of Baltimore Beauties and Beyond, Studies in Classic Album Quilt Appliqué* (1994).

Here are a dozen patterns—fully drafted out and pictured in fabric—for some of the most beautiful fruit and floral borders in the classic Albums. Two magnificent—and relatively simple—enlarged central medallion patterns are included: one from Baltimore, one from "Beyond."

*Papercuts and Plenty—Volume III of Baltimore Beauties and Beyond, Studies in Classic Album Quilt Appliqué,* (1995).

Papercut Appliqué Albums have always been the author's favorite stylistic stream in the antebellum Baltimores. Having saved the best for almost last, Elly both teaches how to design your own blocks and also offers a crescendo of 85 fully drafted patterns to this remarkable series. Intertwining the "how" of the Albums with the "why" of the Albums, Elly includes a beautiful essay on "plenty"—the lush, lifelike, often dimensional bounty of fruit offered up in gratitude by the Classic Albums. As always, she has uncovered exciting new needlework techniques from the old Albums and teaches them here with clarity and beautiful illustrations.

*Stitched in Cloth, Carved in Stone: A Quilter's Odyssey through Centuries of Symbols* (1997).

In this beautifully written and illustrated sequel to *Volume III,* the author picks up the thread of symbolism, which pulled her to Baltimore's Album Quilts in the first place. The book's carefully researched dictionary of antique symbols with an emphasis on fraternal icons and the Language of Flowers draws on original sources. Through a fascinating pictorial comparison between Album block motifs and Victorian gravestones, we gain a sympathetic new understanding of the Album Quiltmakers' world-view and even of our own.

For the modern quiltmaker, the most beloved of symbols stitched in cloth and carved in stone are illustrated by innovatively rich Albums, abloom with the newest rediscoveries in shaded ribbonwork, medallion-making, and dramatic sets. Tying the future to the past, this fascinating volume analyzes what caused the antebellum Baltimore Albums to bloom so profusely, who made these famous quilts, why the style spread so widely, and what brought the Album era to an end? The reader will find, as the author has, that the outward Album journey from past to present, is in fact an inward and on-going voyage of self-discovery.

# C&T PUBLISHING ANNOUNCES

### Revivalist Baltimore Style Album Quilt Contest II and Exhibition

This contest will be hung and judged in 1998. The first three categories are the same as for 1994's C&T Publishing Contest I: (1) Revival of a Classic Style, (2) Reflective of a Particular Life and Times, and (3) Innovative. In addition, there will be new categories, which draw on Elly's more recent books: (4) A Baltimore Basket/Dimensional Bloom Album, (5) A Papercut Album. Entry forms for C&T Publishing's Great Revivalist Baltimore-Style Quilt Contest II are available after September 8, 1995. Send a stamped, self-addressed business-size envelope to C&T Publishing, P.O. Box 1456, Lafayette, CA 94549.

### Call for Teacher Honors

A book is planned to celebrate the 1998 show of contemporary Baltimore-style Album Quilts. In that book, C&T would like to honor the many teachers of the Baltimore style who have made it bloom so gloriously once again in their regions of the country and of the world. If you would like to nominate a teacher for this recognition, please send the teacher's name and address and a short note about the good job she or he has done. C&T would like to hear how those teachers' styles have affected your work and the work of others in your area. Please also include your own name and address, and send it to C&T Publishing, Teacher Honors, P.O. Box 1456, Lafayette, CA 94549. Nominations should be received between January 1 and August 31, 1997.

### Quilting Teacher Resources, Good Ladies of Baltimore Clubs

Did you know that C&T Publishing has great resources for teachers? We'd like to give teachers support. We can send lesson plans, contest news, new book announcements, our catalog with its book news and reviews, and other updates.

How can you form a "Good Ladies of Baltimore, (name of State, Town, or Place) Club"? The idea came from Faye Labanaris who named all from her quilt guild (New Hampshire's Cocheco Quilters, who put on a fabulous Baltimore show one year) and all who had ever been in her Baltimore Album Classes, "Good Ladies of Baltimore, North." That reference appeared beside Faye's book review on the back cover of *Design a Baltimore Album Quilt!* Since then, there have been many inquiries. You can form a Good Ladies of Baltimore Club of your own. But do write to C&T Publishing to register it. Then, if there are enough clubs to warrant mailing you something from Elly (an idea, a pattern, a new class, a challenge), C&T would love to do so!

# OTHER FINE QUILTING BOOKS
# FROM C&T PUBLISHING

*An Amish Adventure*, Roberta Horton
*Appliqué 12 Borders and Medallions!*
    Elly Sienkiewicz
*Appliqué 12 Easy Ways!* Elly Sienkiewicz
*The Art of Silk Ribbon Embroidery*,
    Judith Baker Montano
*Baltimore Album Quilts, Historic Notes and
    Antique Patterns*, Elly Sienkiewicz
*Baltimore Album Revival! Historic Quilts in
    the Making. The Catalog of C&T
    Publishing's Quilt Show and Contest*,
    Elly Sienkiewicz
*Baltimore Beauties and Beyond* (2 Volumes),
    Elly Sienkiewicz
*The Best From Gooseberry Hill: Patterns For
    Stuffed Animals & Dolls*, Kathy Pace
*Buttonhole Stitch Appliqué*, Jean Wells
*A Celebration of Hearts*, Jean Wells and
    Marina Anderson
*Christmas Traditions From the Heart*,
    Margaret Peters
*Christmas Traditions From the Heart, Volume
    Two*, Margaret Peters
*A Colorful Book*, Yvonne Porcella
*Colors Changing Hue*, Yvonne Porcella
*Crazy Quilt Handbook*, Judith Montano
*Crazy Quilt Odyssey*, Judith Montano
*Dating Quilts: A Quick and Easy Reference*,
    Helen Kelley
*Design a Baltimore Album Quilt!*
    Elly Sienkiewicz
*Dimensional Appliqué—Baskets, Blooms &
    Baltimore Borders*, Elly Sienkiewicz
*Elegant Stitches*, Judith Baker Montano
*Fantastic Figures: Ideas & Techniques Using
    the New Clays*, Susanna Oroyan
*14,287 Pieces of Fabrics and Other Poems*,
    Jean Ray Laury
*Friendship's Offering*, Susan McKelvey
*Happy Trails*, Pepper Cory
*Heirloom Machine Quilting*,
    Harriet Hargrave
*Imagery on Fabric*, Jean Ray Laury
*Isometric Perspective*,
    Katie Pasquini-Masopust
*Landscapes & Illusions*, Joen Wolfrom
*The Magical Effects of Color*, Joen Wolfrom
*Mariner's Compass*, Judy Mathieson
*Mastering Machine Appliqué*,
    Harriet Hargrave
*Memorabilia Quilting*, Jean Wells

*The New Lone Star Handbook*, Blanche Young
    and Helen Young Frost
*NSA Series: Bloomin' Creations*, Jean Wells
*NSA Series: Holiday Magic*, Jean Wells
*NSA Series: Hometown*, Jean Wells
*NSA Series: Fans, Hearts, & Folk Art*,
    Jean Wells
*Pattern Play*, Doreen Speckmann
*Perfect Pineapples*, Jane Hall and
    Dixie Haywood
*Picture This*, Jean Wells and
    Marina Anderson
*Pieced Clothing*, Yvonne Porcella
*Pieced Clothing Variations*, Yvonne Porcella
*PQME Series: Basket Quilt*, Jean Wells
*PQME Series: Bear's Paw Quilt*, Jean Wells
*PQME Series: Country Bunny Quilt*,
    Jean Wells
*PQME Series: Milky Way Quilt*, Jean Wells
*PQME Series: Nine-Patch Quilt*, Jean Wells
*PQME Series: Pinwheel Quilt*, Jean Wells
*PQME Series: Sawtooth Star Quilt*,
    Jean Wells
*PQME Series: Stars & Hearts Quilt*,
    Jean Wells
*Patchwork Quilts Made Easy*, Jean Wells
    (with Rodale Press, Inc.)
*Quilts for Fabric Lovers*, Alex Anderson
*Quilts, Quilts, and More Quilts!*
    Diana McClun and Laura Nownes
*Recollections*, Judith Baker Montano
*Soft-Edge Piecing*, Jinny Beyer
*Stitching Free: Easy Machine Pictures*,
    Shirley Nilsson
*Symmetry: A Design System for Quiltmakers*,
    Ruth B. McDowell
*3 Dimensional Design*, Katie Pasquini
*A Treasury of Quilt Labels*, Susan McKelvey
*Virginia Avery's Hats A Heady Affair*
*Virginia Avery's Nifty Neckwear*
*Visions: Quilts, Layers of Excellence*, Quilt
    San Diego
*The Visual Dance: Creating Spectacular
    Quilts*, Joen Wolfrom
*Whimsical Animals*, Miriam Gourley

*For more information write for a free catalog from*
C&T Publishing
P.O. Box 1456
Lafayette, CA 94549
(1-800-284-1114)